# SUNDAY TELEGRAPH
# PATIO
# GARDENING

*Line drawings by Charles Stitt*

*Colour photography by Michael Warren and the author*

*Garden sketches designed and drawn by*
*Kenneth Midgley*

## ROBERT PEARSON

*Mahonia* 'Charity'.

## ROBERT PEARSON

Robert Pearson has been the Gardening Correspondent of the *Sunday Telegraph* since 1971. He was also, until 1985, the Publisher of Collingridge gardening books, and for many years before that the Gardening Editor of the Hamlyn Publishing Group, of which Collingridge forms part.

Trained at some of the finest gardening establishments in Britain, including the Royal Horticultural Society's school of horticulture at Wisley in Surrey, his entire career has been devoted to horticulture, journalism and publishing, apart from war service as a pilot in the Royal Air Force.

He is a Fellow of the Institute of Horticulture and a council member of the Royal National Rose Society.

His much-loved home with large garden is in Hertfordshire.

First published in 1974 by
The SUNDAY TELEGRAPH
Hamlyn Paperback revised edition 1979
Second revised edition 1983
This edition Telegraph Publications 1988
Copyright © SUNDAY TELEGRAPH and
Robert Pearson 1974, 1979, 1983, 1988

ISBN 0 86367 290 6

Telegraph Publications,
Peterborough Court,
At South Quay,
181 Marsh Wall,
London, E14 9SR

*Front cover* A patio garden in Ipswich, 1984, showing how imaginatively a wall of broken paving stones can be used to enhance a small space. *(Photograph supplied by Photos Horticultural)*

Typeset by KMWS Graphics Ltd, London, WC1

Printed and bound in Spain Graficas Estella, S.A.

Pearson, Robert
Patio gardening. – 4th ed.
1. Paved gardens. Ornamental flowering plants
I. Title
635.9'671

ISBN 0-86367-290-6

# Contents

To Diana

# Introduction

I have written this book because I feel deeply that a garden – even the tiniest of gardens – can give infinite pleasure and solace if used to the best advantage.

As land becomes more expensive – an irreversible trend – and gardens consequently become smaller, it is inevitable that

*Pelargoniums (geraniums) and fuchsias have the perfect foil in a backdrop of tender mimosa and bay.*

patio-type gardens will become more and more popular, for not only are these extremely attractive, but they are easy to look after.

Astonishing results can be achieved, even in those of pocket-handkerchief size. This book, however, is by no means solely concerned with the most constricted of patio areas, although these are kept very much in mind. For the patio garden is, in effect, an outdoor room, and rooms can vary in size. Also, it may not take up all your garden area but lead on to features of more traditional design. The possibilities, if not endless, certainly give plenty of scope for the enterprising garden owner.

The wonderful thing about gardening is the scope it gives us to be enterprising – especially in this country. Maybe it is something we give little conscious thought to, but the quite remarkable range of ornamental plants, from trees and shrubs to herbaceous perennials, annuals and bulbs available to the home gardener in Britain gives us all the opportunity to do exciting, even original things with whatever size plot we happen to own. Fortunately, too, the more go-ahead nurseries and seedsmen are always whetting our appetites with new offerings, and trying out some of these always adds zest to one's gardening, even within the confines of a small area such as we are concerned with here.

I would like to thank landscape architect Kenneth Midgley for providing the beautifully executed sketches of patio gardens which you will find on the pages which follow. These show what can be achieved when a sensitive eye is combined with a keen appreciation of plants and their use in settings of the kind we are concerned with. My thanks also to Charles Stitt for the outstanding line drawings of plants and, in some cases, garden features, which so splendidly set the scene and to Michael Warren for providing the majority of the colour photographs. Like Mr Midgley they are masters of their diverse arts. The photographs on the following pages were taken by myself: 39, 50-1, 55 (insert), 74, 83, 86, 90-1, 98-9, 122, 127, 130-1, 134-5, 139, 146, 154, 158 and 159.

Having said that, it only remains for me to express the hope that this book will prove helpful to you in your patio gardening – both in the planning and the execution.

*Robert Pearson*

# 1. Why a patio garden?

Why a patio garden? I can best answer this question by contrasting two gardens which, although of quite different character, both basically presented their owners with the same problems and opportunities.

The first lay behind a terraced house in the suburb of a large city and consisted of a plot perhaps 60ft (18m) long by 20ft (6m) wide. It had possibilities, for the light was by no means bad, there were walls to grow things on and the site was sheltered – but little had been done. A patchy lawn was surrounded on three sides by a rather sad-looking border filled in desultory fashion with a motley collection of plants. Opportunities had been missed, though I suppose even this garden gave its owner satisfaction of a kind.

The other garden was attached to a semi-detached home in an urban area, and the small corner site had been turned into a charming patio-type garden by the skilful use of plants and paving. Everything was perfectly in scale.

A small cherry tree in one corner led the eye round to a trellis-topped fence over which the tangled growth of *Clematis montana* spread to hide effectively other houses from view. Climbing roses enveloped the garage wall, flowering and foliage shrubs and perennials were growing in plant beds, and less permanent plants in a few containers stood on the paving slabs which linked with other features to give the garden balance and an air of studied calm. It was, to my mind, the kind of garden a family could live with and enjoy for many a year.

This garden had no eating-out area, but that is something which many patio gardens can incorporate if you have a taste for such delights. Can I use this as an example, though, of the necessity for foresight in garden planning? What you must have with an eating-out area is easy access to the house and kitchen, otherwise the continual to-ing and fro-ing will soon become an irritant and a bore. On-the-spot barbecue facilities are fun for parties but are not the kind of thing you want for everyday living.

The first site I mentioned could with little trouble have been

9

turned into quite a pleasant garden of conventional design. But with a good boundary wall, not high enough to cut out light, what an opportunity had been lost to turn it into a patio garden of real character and charm.

No plot is too small for this. After all, just think what countless plant lovers manage to achieve with a balcony garden or even a few window boxes. Imagination and enthusiasm are more important in gardening than space.

Why not go out into your garden now and cast an eye over the assets you already have? Perhaps you have good walls or close-board fencing on a couple of sides of your property, providing shelter and privacy and all kinds of opportunities to grow interesting plants. Perhaps there is a tree of suitable proportions which could form the focal point of a completely new design, or, say, you have a paved area already which could form the basis for a patio garden.

With any of these advantages the battle is already on its way to being won. But don't be deterred if you have to start from scratch.

Above all, be practical, and decide very early on just how much money you are prepared to spend. That is really the crux of the matter – the key to everything in the end.

Making a patio garden can also be a time-consuming business but, once made and planted, it is far more labour-saving than a conventional garden.

# 2. Elements of Design

Gardening is something one should never be dogmatic about – it is often so much a matter of taste and opinion – but that will not deter me from saying that the key to success in patio garden making is simplicity of design. That is true of any garden making, but the limited scale of a patio garden makes it even more important.

So often too many features are included, too many plants are crammed into a small area with unsatisfactory or even disastrous results (which is not to say that you cannot 'mass' plants successfully if they have a basic affinity).

Unobtrusive paving, a small flowering tree of delicate outline, a few choice climbing plants and some plant containers filled with gay geraniums, long-flowering fuchsias or hydrangeas may be all that is needed to create a garden of delight. But then, other features might be far better – it depends on the circumstances. I hope that in the pages which follow you will be able to pick and choose, from the features and plants described, those which will suit you best.

**Planning your patio**
If garden planning does not come easily to you I would suggest that you seek early advice from a professional garden designer or landscape architect, if only to get him or her to draw up a plan to which you can afterwards work. A trained eye would quickly pick out the good things about the site which could be exploited, and, just as important, advise on how less favourable aspects of it could be played down. But if you seek advice, do get an estimate in advance so that you know what your financial commitment will be.

One of the first things you must secure in your garden is shelter and a modicum of privacy, for there is no pleasure in being chilled to the bone, even on a sunny day, or in trying to relax in the public eye.

Although in a patio garden, with its space limitations, hedges are not always a practical proposition, they should not be ruled out altogether. A yew hedge which can be kept trimmed to a foot thick, for example, can be a delightful feature, but in general hedges take up far too much lateral room and draw too much goodness from the soil.

This plot, 30ft (9m) wide by 50ft (15m) long, is backed by a neighbouring building and enclosed on two sides by walls. (In other circumstances these last could easily be high fences.) Basically, the design takes the form of a pattern of rectangles outlined in a hard-fired brick and these interlocking shapes, together with the plantings and the garden furniture, give the whole garden a real feeling of being an outdoor room. Again, the trees – these could be something like Acer ginnala, Malus robusta 'Yellow Siberian', or one of the smaller-growing flowering cherries – balance the design and give the garden a different level of interest. The grass "carpet" makes a useful sitting-out area and contrasts pleasingly with the paving around it. However, if more colour is needed, this minute lawn could be a bed with flowering plants or such plants could replace the pool.

This design illustrates how the simplest of shapes, allied to restrained planting, can please the eye and result in a garden which many home owners would find sympathetic and – very important – continue to enjoy over many years.

Brick walls can be delightful to look at and very sympathetic to plants, but they may, regretfully, have to be ruled out on account of cost, so one comes back to fencing of one kind or another. Wood is by far the nicest choice: best of all, close-board fencing or the overlap type which makes a good surface to grow plants on or against. But whatever your choice, don't make the screen so high that you cut out the light. Remember, too, that although you have to guard against chill winds both for the sake of the plants and yourself, a garden which is too much enclosed becomes almost too hot on very sunny summer days.

If you have a patio which leads into a main garden area, then open-work screen walling in precast concrete can, in short sections, provide just the right kind of division between the two – not too heavy, not too insubstantial.

House and garden walls in towns, exposed to years of industrial pollution, can take on depressingly dark shades, and when this happens it is well worth while colour-washing parts at least in white or perhaps a pastel shade. This will give the whole garden a quite different appearance and provide a congenial backdrop for plants.

Paving of one kind or another which will take the wear of continual traffic is, of course, a vital feature of any patio garden. Its quality sets the tone of the whole plot. Real stone paving or patterned bricks – of the special hard-fired quality necessary to withstand exposure to moisture and low temperatures – make surfaces of great aesthetic appeal, but it can be costly these days to cover even a small area.

Usually, it will be a case of opting for one of the proprietary brands of precast concrete paving slabs which are so freely available – and very attractive some of these can be. They come in various shapes and sizes, textures and finishes, and in a range of colours to meet most requirements and tastes. You will find them on display at builders' merchants, garden centres and major flower shows like Chelsea. It is worth taking the trouble to find just what you want.

Sometimes local councils sell off old paving slabs which are surplus to their requirements, and bargain lots can occasionally be obtained in this way. If it is of interest to you it is certainly worth inquiring at your local council offices, even if the answer is likely to be No.

It is often a good idea to break up the uniformity of paved areas by incorporating patterned areas of granite setts or cobbles, although it is best to keep the latter away from areas where you will walk frequently as they can be slippery in wet weather. Lovely effects can be achieved by making up simple designs in this way, especially around specimen trees.

Stepping-stones – circular, square or rectangular and made of artificial stone – can look delightful in association with appropriate

plantings. Indeed, they can be strong enough to be a design feature of some importance in a garden of the dimensions we are thinking of.

It might be helpful to know that if you intend using concrete in your garden, whether in the form of paving, steps, open-work screen walling, raised plant beds or the like, that the British Cement Association publish an excellent well-illustrated 28-page booklet 'Concrete Round Your House and Garden', which gives detailed advice on concrete as a material and how to make maximum use of it in the garden. It is available from garden centres, builders merchants and specialist retail stores or direct from Publications Sales, British Cement Association, Wexham Springs, Slough SL3 6PL, price £1.00, postage included.

One thing I would not use concrete for myself, unless I were getting a professional job done, is making a small pool, of the kind of size suitable for most patio settings. It is much easier nowadays to buy a glass-fibre pool ''off the shelf'', or a plastic pool liner for which – apart from the precautions I detail on p. 108 – there is little more preparation than the digging of a hole of the required size, shape and depth. Concrete pools are vulnerable to frost damage, especially if home-made mixtures are not of quite the right consistency or if they are too thinly applied to withstand the worst that the weather can throw up in its most arctic-like moods.

A small water feature complete with water-lilies and other aquatic plants – not too many – can add great charm to a patio garden, especially if edged with stonework effectively to hide from view the material of which the pool itself is made. It will be an even greater source of pleasure if you install a small fountain. Under-water lighting sets are also becoming very popular, and these can provide quite impressive effects. A two-lamp set, complete with low-voltage transformer, can be bought for quite a modest sum.

An interesting variation on this theme is to have the pool only partially sunk in the ground, and surround it with a low wall which can be used as a seat. For this again you could use precast concrete blocks and slabs.

*A path of concrete paving with cobbles used to provide a variation in form and texture, can be pleasing to the eye.*

## Plants and planting

Plants in paving are always attractive, and I have suggested some suitable subjects for such a feature on pp. 144 to 146. Beds and borders for plants should not be overdone in a garden of this kind, for you must keep that essential quality I mentioned earlier, balance, constantly in mind; but within those limits a great deal can be achieved. I would always myself use a good leavening of plants with attractive foliage or form as well as those notable for the beauty of their flowers, so that there is the best possible spread of interest throughout the year. The flowering periods of most plants are relatively short while foliage and form can be enjoyed for at least half the year, and all the year round in the case of evergreens.

Of course, there are plants which possess two, and some even all three of these attributes -shrubs like *Paeonia lutea ludlowii* and *Mahonia* 'Charity' and perennials like *Alchemilla mollis*, the lady's mantle, the hostas and *Euphorbia characias* to name but a few.

Herbaceous perennial plants with special qualities certainly find a place in beds or borders, and perhaps some annuals to use as colourful 'fillers' in summer. Some climbing plants, too, these perhaps being grown on pillars to complement those grown on the house walls, fences and so on.

A fairly recent innovation is the raised bed, designed to help the elderly and the infirm to continue to garden effectively without bending down. A joy to many people certainly, but what I want to stress now is the value of the raised bed as a design feature in its own right. A raised bed in a paved area makes a splendid home for rock plants and dwarf bulbous plants, not to mention a dwarf conifer or two, miniature roses and small-growing shrubs like *Hebe pinguifolia* 'Pagei'; *Spiraea japonica* 'Alpina'; the dwarf willow, *Salix apoda*; and heathers like the lime tolerant, ruby-red, winter-flowering *Erica carnea* 'Myretoun Ruby' and, for summer flowering (and lime-free soil), the magenta *E. cinerea* 'Stephen Davis'. Such a feature can be a source of pleasure during every season of the year. A bed raised just a few inches above the level of the garden can also be valuable, strengthening the overall design.

Small-growing rock and bulbous plants can also be grown most attractively in trough gardens. Real stone troughs, though, of the kind one used to see in every farmyard, and the lovely old stone sinks which used to catch the overflow from village pumps, are becoming extremely difficult, indeed almost impossible, to obtain.

In the final analysis it is usually a case of making do with a trough made from reconstituted stone or perhaps a glazed domestic sink, although even these are not so readily available nowadays. Sinks can be effectively treated to hide the shiny surface, or one can mask the glazing with trailing plants. What

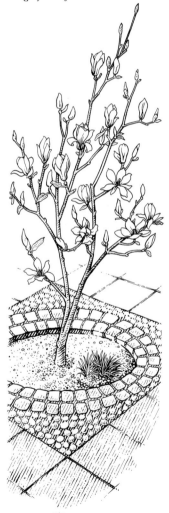

*Paving, brickwork and cobbles frame a shrub or small tree in a delightful way.*

17

you should *not* do is to attempt to grow alpines in plastic containers, which dry out far too quickly in hot weather for the good of the occupants.

Plant containers, whether they are large tubs, bowls and the like or window-boxes, have an important part to play in the patio garden, primarily, of course, as receptacles for housing short-term, seasonal plants; but not exclusively so, by any means. Numerous shrubs can be grown on a permanent basis in this way as well as fruit trees (see Chapter Thirteen) and perennials like the phormiums, if you take the trouble to top-dress the soil annually and generally look after them as I describe on p. 107.

What possibilities flowering bulbs, corms and tubers offer the patio gardener! Apart from the daffodils and tulips in their almost bewildering array, there are the hyacinths and small treasures like snowdrops, dwarf irises, grape hyacinths, eranthises and scillas, the crocuses, and easy lilies like the beautiful *Lilium regale*, all of which can delight the eye in the kind of intimate garden setting we are considering. In Chapter Nine I take a close look at the possibilities open to the patio gardener with a liking for this group of plants.

It may sound a little bizarre to suggest growing vegetables and fruit in the patio garden, and naturally I am not suggesting that this is going to fill your larder or deep freeze unit to over-flowing. But it is surprising, nevertheless, what produce can, on occasions, be raised on a small piece of ground or in plant containers. Even a small number of outdoor tomatoes, for instance, can be very prolific in a good summer, or you could grow runner beans or those delicious little Courgette marrows as well as lettuces, radishes and spring onions. Raspberries, too, can be grown in plant containers, strawberries in pots and if you have a bed at the foot of a north-facing wall there is a chance to make use of it by training a Morello cherry against it.

Trained fruit trees can look very attractive, and you could even find room for an espalier-trained apple or pear or a few of the same fruits cordon-trained. Even, perhaps, a so-called "family tree" in which three varieties of desert apples or three of pears are grafted on one bush-trained specimen (see p. 161).

Grass has a minor part to play in the patio garden, if indeed it has any part to play at all, but even a small ribbon of close-textured turf can be extremely effective if it is integrated into the overall design with care (see the designs on pp. 13, 64, 124 and 141). The fresh green colouring is soothing to the eye throughout the year and there is no better foil, in my opinion, for a multi-coloured border of flowers. Even a strip, say, of 4ft (1.3m) wide can have relevance in a small patio garden, but it must have a well-coiffured look if it is not to appear incongruous. Apart from regular trimming in the growing season, it must be fed and watered as circumstances demand.

Phormium tenax *cultivar*

A suggestion for the treatment of an area measuring only 20ft (6m) across and 25ft (7.5m) deep facing a bare wall and with flanking walls on both sides. Evergreen shrubs give the garden form and the two trees atmosphere, and this winter scene illustrates the point that the tracery of bare branches, as provided by the birch on the left, or even a winter-flowering cherry (Prunus subhirtella 'Autumnalis') as shown on the right, is a pleasure not to be under-rated. Low-growing ground-cover plants come into their own in such a setting, and need little attention. The stepping stones are discs of artificial stone, and the curve these describe, echoing the curve of the plant bed, give this patio garden a certain dramatic quality.

A small piece of statuary can add much to the beauty of a patio garden if it is well executed and used as a focal point of the design. I have seen beautiful effects created by framing such features with the foliage of shrubs and so on. Good statuary is not easy to come by – it may take time and patience to find what you want.

### Choosing furniture and containers

If you intend to make a lot of use of the patio as an outdoor room, then it is worth taking considerable trouble over choosing garden furniture. Whether wood, metal or plastic is a matter of preference, and dependent to some extent on the kind of garden you have planned. High-quality wooden furniture – made of some really durable wood like teak or iroko – has an air of solidity which metal sometimes lacks, but if the whole atmosphere of the garden radiates lightness and grace then metal furniture may be just what is needed to set it off. Aluminium alloy furniture, in particular, can be very pleasing, likewise nylon-coated steel furniture with polyethylene seats. I find cane furniture very pleasing too in this kind of setting, but you have to have somewhere to store it when it is not in use.

Don't underestimate the aesthetic importance of containers. Like paving and garden furniture, these can help set the general tone of the whole garden. The severely clean lines of, say, a moulded asbestos-cement container or a concrete bowl may be just right in one setting, whereas in another setting something with more ornamentation, like the lovely glass fibre reproductions of period urns, vases, etc., one can buy, might be more pleasing and appropriate. These last can be extraordinarily reminiscent of the originals. Again, in a rather homely setting, hardwood containers, either with their natural finish or painted, the better to show off the flowers they will contain, might be a more suitable choice. Have a good look round and consider all the options before making up your mind.

### A plan of campaign

Indeed, get your ideas thoroughly sorted out before you commit yourself to anything, whether plants, materials or furniture.

Then get the basic construction work completed as quickly as possible and take your time, if need be, over completing the planting and furnishing. Spreading the financial outlay in this way makes it possible to do rather more ambitious things than might otherwise be possible. It is a great convenience nowadays to be able to obtain from garden centres many good garden plants as container-grown specimens for immediate planting at any time of the year, so long as the weather is suitable. It means that you can take things calmly and gradually build up the kind of garden you want.

Lilium regale *(see p. 18)*.

I mentioned earlier the importance of foliage and form – shapes in other words. Now a word about colour which it is always a joy to see used in gardens with sensitivity. What you need to keep firmly in mind is that green, in its infinite gradations, is always restful to the eye; the red end of the spectrum has just the opposite effect; blue is a lovely cool colour to enjoy on a warm summer day, while yellow is the colour which lifts the spirits, even when the sky is cloud-wracked. Go out into the garden on a dull day at any time of year and you will find that it is the yellow of flower, leaf or berry which introduces a joyous note. Grey foliage and white flowers will both give the garden a touch of sophistication if deployed with artistry. This is something, I am glad to say, which is being increasingly recognised by the gardening fraternity.

So, as I said at the start, keep the basic design simple. Use strong colours with discretion, especially those extrovert reds and oranges. Try to make different features relate to one another so that you have a unified garden rather than a jumble of disparate parts. In that way you will capture the peace and serenity which is the greatest gift that a garden – any garden, patio or otherwise – can give to its owner. Achieve that, and the patio will be a part of the home to which you will gravitate on every possible occasion.

*Statuary and foliage combined can form the focal point of the design (see p. 21).*

# 3. Climbing, Wall and Other Shrubs

Ornamental shrubs of one kind or another are the backbone of the modern garden, whatever its size. They are available in almost bewildering array, and provided one takes account of their special needs – if they have any – they are the easiest of plants to look after. An annual spring mulch, perhaps a little pruning, although this is not always necessary, and watering in the driest periods are just about all the attention many of them need. And look what they give us in return!

They are a natural choice for the patio garden, for a few, selected with care, and with perhaps a small tree to provide a different level of interest, form the framework for the whole design. Climbing shrubs, too, and non-climbing shrubs which are particularly well suited for growing against walls or fences, have a special importance.

Cistus skanbergii

There is something else to consider as well, if you are the adventurous type of gardener I hope you are, and that is the opportunity your patio garden gives you to grow shrubs and other plants which are on the borderline of hardiness. By definition a patio garden is an enclosed garden and that must mean that it provides plants with a greater degree of warmth and shelter than it is possible to find in a more open situation. Use it to the full. There are so many plants of excellence which fall in this category from cistuses (or rock roses) like *Cistus skanbergii*, a lovely 3ft (1m) tall and wide shrub which bears its papery-textured pink flowers in early summer, to sun-loving hebes like 'Great Orme' and 'Autumn Glory' – low-growing, evergreen shrubs which bear pink and violet-blue flower spikes respectively, the first from early summer, the second from July to autumn. Warm south- or west-facing walls provide an ideal background for things like *Abutilon megapotamicum* and *A. vitifolium* 'Veronica Tennant', the very showy *Fremontodendron* California Glory' (which you may know under its former, and less clumsy, name *Fremontia* 'Californian Glory'), the passion flower, *Passiflora caerulea*, and much else besides. More about these in a moment, and others which could give you great pleasure over the years.

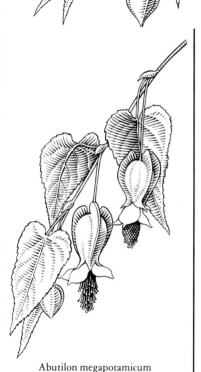

Abutilon megapotamicum
*(see p. 23)*.

So, don't always play safe and go for absolute reliability whatever the weather, for you miss so much enjoyment that way. Accept the challenge. One thing nobody can do is to define exactly the degree of hardiness of any plant. It depends on so many different factors, from the microclimate to which the plant is subjected (aspect, light availability and the degree of warmth and shelter provided) to the soil conditions you are able to offer and, yes, imponderables. We all know of occasions when a plant has failed miserably in one place yet romped away in another not, on the face of it, very much different. It is that kind of thing which makes gardening so exciting.

**Planting and cultivation**
Before discussing specific plants, a word or two about more general considerations, including planting and basic cultivation. It is fatally easy to be so mesmerised by the charms of some particular plant as to disregard completely the conditions it needs to succeed. It is a trap to avoid. If a plant needs lots of sunshine or, conversely, light shade, or if it needs an acid soil rather than one which is alkaline, do not expect it to put up with quite the wrong conditions without complaint. It won't.

Container-grown plants, as I have said, are a great convenience, making the whole year a planting season. The reason is, of course, that when you remove a plant from a container you cause very little disturbance to the root system and it rapidly settles down again.

But nursery stock lifted from the open ground is a different proposition. It is lifted for dispatch only at the traditional planting seasons, the time, of course, when re-establishment in the garden is easiest and the least strain is put on the plant's resources. So with deciduous trees and shrubs it is from late October or early November, after leaf fall, until March, except when excessive wet or frost and snow make this impossible. With evergreens the best times of all for planting are from late September until late October and from the beginning of April to May; but, of course, you can plant in mild spells in winter if you take all the normal precautions.

The two optimum times I have mentioned are so good because the soil is reasonably warm at those times; yet the sun is not so hot that it will cause excessive transpiration through the leaves. Nor with a bit of luck will strong winds cause heavy transpiration either at those times of the year. It is not always realised that wind is as much an enemy as hot sunshine to evergreen shrubs whose roots have not yet started to function again efficiently in their new home, for unlike deciduous shrubs they have no resting period. For that reason they are much more tricky to re-establish.

If your plants arrive when the weather is unsuitable for planting because of frost, snow or heavy rain, leave the root wrapping on but take away the top-growth covering and place in some cool, frost-proof place until conditions improve; or heel them in in a specially opened up trench out of doors, just covering the roots with soil and firming with the heel. The latter treatment is to be preferred, if the bad weather lasts for more than a week.

A few other pre-planting needs. Cut off cleanly any damaged roots, just above the break. Make the planting hole just a little larger than the roots at their full spread, assuming that they are not in a soil 'ball'. Fork over the bottom of the hole and cover it with a thin layer of garden compost (if you have it available) before adding a little top soil. The hole should be of such a depth that the shrub will be at the same level when planted as it was when growing in the nursery – something you should be able to check easily as the soil mark on the stem is usually clearly visible.

Place the shrub in position – after you have put in a stout stake, if support is needed early on – and work good quality top soil in among the roots with the fingers, or, if there is a root "ball", around this. Firm with the foot, add more top soil, firm and repeat this procedure until the soil is slightly above the surrounding soil level. This is to allow for the small amount of sinking there will inevitably be as the soil settles down.

If the wind is a problem, and it should not be in a sheltered patio garden, it is always a good thing to shield newly planted evergreens for a time, on the windward side, with a temporary screen of hessian or polythene sheeting, supported by stakes. This will cut down considerably the loss of moisture through the leaves caused by transpiration. Help the evergreens all you can, too, in the post-planting period by watering as necessary and spraying over the leaves in the late afternoon.

Mulching around shrubs with peat, composted bark or garden compost, after the soil has had a chance to warm up in spring, will greatly help to conserve soil moisture during dry periods – but make sure, by periodically drawing back the mulch, that the soil is not dry underneath. Water, if necessary.

## Clematis
Consider wall plants in the context of the typical patio garden and one's thoughts immediately fly to roses and clematis, both of which are available in wide variety. Both, of course, put on an impressive display, and they often make the loveliest of com-

panions. Ceanothus and pyracantha are other shrubs which make ideal companions for clematis.

Roses are dealt with in a separate chapter (see p. 79), so I shall say no more about them now, but turn your attention to the clematis, which have so much to offer the gardener between spring and autumn. From the earliest flowering species like the rather tender creamy-white *C. armandii* (an evergreen species and also needing a warm home), through the large-flowered hybrids to those yellow-flowered species *C. orientalis* and *C. tangutica*, which bring an end to the season, they provide so much of interest.

A special joy, I always find, is the May-June-flowering *C. montana*, the vigorous species so much grown in its rose-pink variety *rubens*. And indeed it is a lovely sight for a few weeks with its mass of blooms set off by bronzy-purple foliage and in the vigorous way so typical of the montanas reaching up to a height of 30ft (9m) or more on wall or roof. But I myself prefer the magnificent white-flowered *C. montana grandiflora*, dazzling in the full flush of it flowering with its myriad blooms set among fresh green foliage. Another beautiful variety is the soft pink 'Elizabeth', and many gardeners have an affection for the large-flowered 'Tetrarose', which has mauvish-pink flowers and bronzy-green leaves. These *montana* varieties will succeed on a wall of any aspect and they are delightful shrubs for the patio garden.

Like the large-flowered hybrids, *C. montana* and its cultivars, as well as other clematis species, like to have their roots in cool shade and their tops in sun. This is not difficult to arrange. You either grow leafy perennials around their base or just lay flat stones on the soil around the stems. Acid and alkaline soils suit them equally well. (You can obtain simple soil-testing kits from garden stores incidentally to determine the lime content of your soil, for when plants do have specific needs.)

Clematis are versatile, too. A vigorous species like *montana* is excellent for growing on trees as well as walls, and the less strong growing hybrids with their large distinctive flowers are ideal for pillars and fences as well as walls.

Let's start with early flowerers. It goes without saying that any climber which flowers in late winter (between January and March) must be a valuable acquisition, and that *Clematis cirrhosa* certainly is, especially in its form *balearica*, the fern-leaved clematis as it is called. The dark-green leaves turn bronze in winter and provide a telling foil for the pendant, pale greenish-yellow blooms which are marked reddish-purple on the inside of the sepals. In ideal conditions it will grow 15ft (4.5m) tall, but usually it is considerably less than that.

The very handsome *C. armandii* also grows up to 15ft (4.5m) tall, even 20ft (6m) on occasions, and what an asset it is at all times

Clematis tangutica
*(see p. 29)*

**Opposite:** *Apart from the fuchsias, this planting scene relies entirely on foliage effect through the wall-scaling* Hedera helix *'Goldheart', spotted aucuba and* Elaeagnus pungens maculata.

Clematis macropetala

with its showy, glossy green leaves, each consisting of three leaflets up to 6in (15cm) long. It is a sight to see in March and April when the large clusters of creamy-white flowers are present. Much valued, too is its cultivar 'Apple Blossom', in which the flowers are pink-tinged. There is also a pure white cultivar named 'Snowdrift'. I would emphasise, however, that really warm, sun-drenched and sheltered conditions are needed by *C. armandii* and its cultivars. Likewise, *C. cirrhosa* and its cultivar *balearica*.

Growing 6ft (2m) or rather more tall is *C. alpina* with beautiful, smallish blue to purple, lantern-shaped flowers in April. It is an excellent choice for clothing a fence and, a not unimportant consideration, proved in recent arctic winter spells, the hardiest of all the clematis. Two excellent cultivars are the blue 'Frances Rivis' and 'White Moth' with double, white blooms. Another is 'Ruby' with purplish-pink blooms.

Another very beautiful clematis which always intrigues me with its pendant bell-shaped, semi-double flowers is *C. macropetala*, a species from Northern China and Siberia. These flowers are violet-blue in colour and are borne in May and June. A height of 10ft (3m) may be achieved but it is often rather less and it makes a splendid adornment for a fence or, as I once saw it grown, festooning a large garden ornament. 'Markham's Pink' is a colour variant of equal attraction.

The early, large-flowered hybrids make marvellous plants for growing in large containers or tubs, and I have more to say about these and other clematis suitable for such a role on p. 116. That splendid old cultivar 'Nelly Moser' belongs here; how attractive it is with its flowers of mauvish-pink, each sepal of that colour overlaid with a carmine bar. So does the lovely lavender-blue, cream-stamened 'Lasurstern', 'Bee's Jubilee', deep pink with a rose-pink bar on the sepals, and purple 'The President'. All of these flower in May and June with a second flush later in summer. Indeed, 'The President' is usually carrying blooms from May until September. There are many more cultivars to choose from.

Following these in flower, from June or July to August or September, are the mid-season cultivars like 'Marie Boisselot', pure gleaming white in colour and with cream stamens, 'W. E. Gladstone', lavender coloured and with purplish-red stamens, and 'Henryi', a hybrid with creamy-white pointed sepals and brown stamens.

The Jackmanii and Viticella hybrids are the rearguard, so to speak, of the large-flowered clematis, flowering from July to late August or September although a few of the first-mentioned type like the striking carmine-red 'Ville de Lyon' (which has bright yellow stamens) and the fine magenta-red 'Ernest Markham' are in flower by June to give a very long period of colour. It would be unthinkable not to mention also the violet-purple 'Jackmanii

Superba', for that is probably the most widely grown of all clematis.

With heights of up to 15ft (4.5m) in the case of the Jackmanii hybrids and 10ft (3m) or less in respect of the Viticella kinds – white-flowered, dark stamened 'Alba Luxurians' is one of note, the extraordinary velvety, deep purple 'Royal Velours' another – there is a lot of scope for enterprise in their display. The Viticella hybrids have a good colour range, do not suffer from that so far intractable trouble, clematis wilt (for which there is no cure at present although one may be on the way) and have small to medium-sized flowers which stand up well to exposure to bad weather.

The strong-growing mid-season flowering hybrids, the Jackmanii and Viticella hybrids and later-flowering species like *C. orientalis* and *C. tangutica* with heights of around 20ft (6m) are ideal for climbing through trees and shrubs in patio settings.

*Clematis orientalis* and *C. tangutica* flower in late summer and early autumn. In addition to the yellow flowers – bell-shaped and with very thick sepals in the case of *C. orientalis*, lantern-shaped in the case of *C. tangutica* – there is the attraction of the handsome, silky, silvery seed heads which both species carry in early autumn. You can expect both to make a delightful show against a wall.

With so many types of clematis – and there are plenty I have not even mentioned, all splendid garden plants in their own right – some logical system of classification is imperative and, following talks with clematis specialist Raymond Evison, whose knowledge of these flowers is unrivalled, I am following, with his permission, the eminently sensible scheme which he has adopted.

His classification is as follows:

Group 1 – Evergreen clematis, including *C. cirrhosa* and *C. armandii; C. alpina, C. macropetala* and *C. montana.*
Group 2 – Early, large-flowered hybrids and mid-season large-flowered hybrids.
Group 3 – Jackmanii, later-flowering, large-flowered hybrids, late-flowering species and their small-flowered cultivars, including *C. orientalis* and *C. tangutica,* which I discuss above.

Group 1 clematis need light pruning just after flowering; Group 2 should have dead and weak growth cut out and be cut back to a strong pair of leaf axil buds in February or March; Group 3 should be hard pruned down to just above the base of the previous season's stems in late February or March.

I have written at length about clematis because these climbers have such relevance to patio-gardening conditions. They can be hugely enjoyable.

### Wisteria and honeysuckle

One of the best wall plants for a patio garden is the wisteria, always attractive when in leaf and magnificent in early summer when it is bearing its glorious racemes of fragrant, lilac-blue flowers. But you must be able to give it a warm position, facing south or south-west. It will, of course, climb to 30ft (9m) or more.

What you can do, though, if you haven't the room to let one climb is to have a standard specimen and grow it in a special planting area in the paving. I have several trained this way in a

*Cultivars of* Clematis alpina, *like 'Ruby' shown here, are a glorious sight in April (see p. 28).*

grass setting and they are a delight with their branches twisting themselves into the most appealing oriental-looking shapes. They can, however, be quite expensive to buy, because of the training involved and few nurseries have them on offer.

There are two types of wisteria – the Chinese, mauve or lilac-coloured *Wisteria sinensis*, of which there are white and purple forms, and the Japanese *W. floribunda*, usually offered in its cultivar 'Macrobotrys', which is notable for the length of the bluish-lilac racemes of flowers. These can be as much as 3ft (1m) long. This also has a white-flowered form, *alba*, which can look

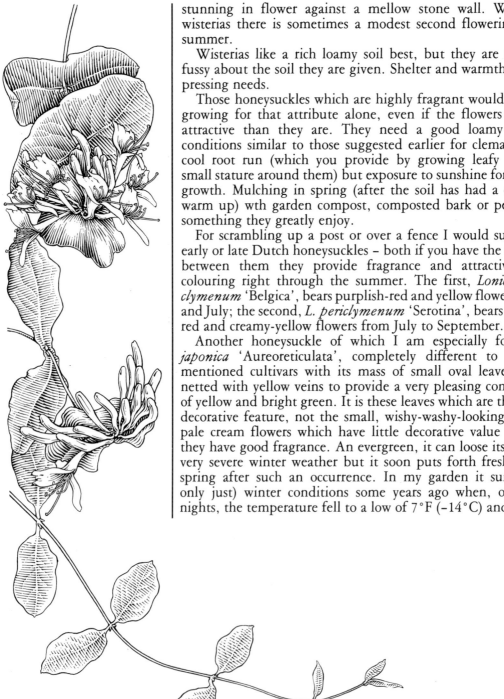

stunning in flower against a mellow stone wall. With these wisterias there is sometimes a modest second flowering in late summer.

Wisterias like a rich loamy soil best, but they are not really fussy about the soil they are given. Shelter and warmth are more pressing needs.

Those honeysuckles which are highly fragrant would be worth growing for that attribute alone, even if the flowers were less attractive than they are. They need a good loamy soil and conditions similar to those suggested earlier for clematis, i.e. a cool root run (which you provide by growing leafy plants of small stature around them) but exposure to sunshine for their top growth. Mulching in spring (after the soil has had a chance to warm up) wth garden compost, composted bark or peat is also something they greatly enjoy.

For scrambling up a post or over a fence I would suggest the early or late Dutch honeysuckles – both if you have the room, for between them they provide fragrance and attractive flower colouring right through the summer. The first, *Lonicera periclymenum* 'Belgica', bears purplish-red and yellow flowers in June and July; the second, *L. periclymenum* 'Serotina', bears purplish-red and creamy-yellow flowers from July to September.

Another honeysuckle of which I am especially fond is *L. japonica* 'Aureoreticulata', completely different to the last-mentioned cultivars with its mass of small oval leaves heavily netted with yellow veins to provide a very pleasing combination of yellow and bright green. It is these leaves which are the plant's decorative feature, not the small, wishy-washy-looking white to pale cream flowers which have little decorative value although they have good fragrance. An evergreen, it can loose its leaves in very severe winter weather but it soon puts forth fresh ones in spring after such an occurrence. In my garden it survived (if only just) winter conditions some years ago when, on several nights, the temperature fell to a low of 7°F (–14°C) and its com-

Lonicera tellmanniana

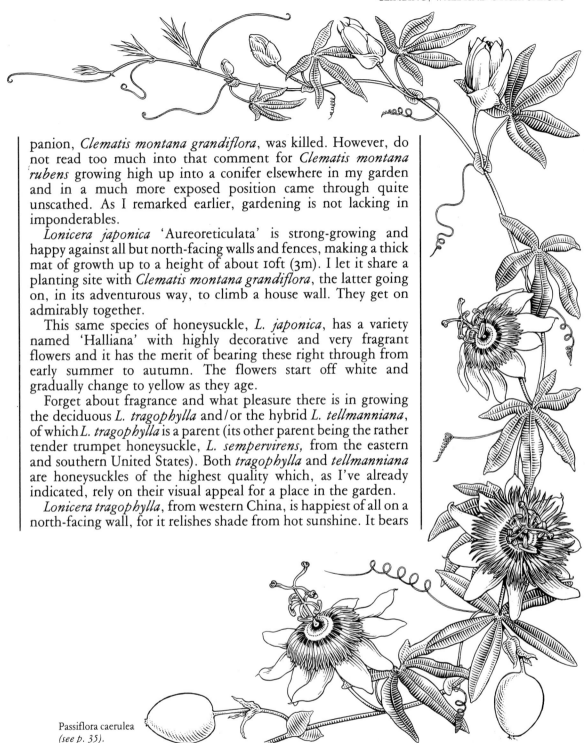

panion, *Clematis montana grandiflora*, was killed. However, do not read too much into that comment for *Clematis montana rubens* growing high up into a conifer elsewhere in my garden and in a much more exposed position came through quite unscathed. As I remarked earlier, gardening is not lacking in imponderables.

*Lonicera japonica* 'Aureoreticulata' is strong-growing and happy against all but north-facing walls and fences, making a thick mat of growth up to a height of about 10ft (3m). I let it share a planting site with *Clematis montana grandiflora*, the latter going on, in its adventurous way, to climb a house wall. They get on admirably together.

This same species of honeysuckle, *L. japonica*, has a variety named 'Halliana' with highly decorative and very fragrant flowers and it has the merit of bearing these right through from early summer to autumn. The flowers start off white and gradually change to yellow as they age.

Forget about fragrance and what pleasure there is in growing the deciduous *L. tragophylla* and/or the hybrid *L. tellmanniana*, of which *L. tragophylla* is a parent (its other parent being the rather tender trumpet honeysuckle, *L. sempervirens,* from the eastern and southern United States). Both *tragophylla* and *tellmanniana* are honeysuckles of the highest quality which, as I've already indicated, rely on their visual appeal for a place in the garden.

*Lonicera tragophylla*, from western China, is happiest of all on a north-facing wall, for it relishes shade from hot sunshine. It bears

Passiflora caerulea
*(see p. 35).*

the most beautiful narrowly-cylindrical, bright yellow flowers in clusters of 10 to 20 in June and July on a plant which climbs to a height of 15ft (4.5m) or so. *L. tellmanniana* – deciduous like *tragophylla* – grows to a similar height and has a similar flowering period, bearing bright yellow flowers which are tipped with bronze, a colour which suffuses the flowers at the bud stage.

### More choice climbers

The climber everybody wants to grow, though, if they have the right conditions, is the passion flower, *Passiflora caerulea* – and no wonder when one thinks of the extraordinary beauty of those complex flowers whose various parts are supposed to represent Christ's Passion: a glorious amalgam of white petals, purplish-blue corona, and other shades as well. These flowers can be enjoyed for most of the summer and into autumn on a climber at least 15ft (4.5m) tall. For this, a warm, sunny wall is a necessity, and in good years rich yellow fruit will also be produced. If it gets cut back in winter there is every chance, too, in favoured gardens, that it will break again in the following spring.

A superbly decorative ivy for the patio is the Persian ivy, *Hedera colchica,* in its variegated form 'Dentata Variegata'. Large, heart-shaped leaves which are a mixture of green, grey and creamy-white – yellow, too, when young – give this climber real value as a patio plant, and it loves to trail along the ground as well as climb. Another colourful variant is *H. colchica* 'Sulphur Heart', (or 'Paddy's Pride' as it is also called) which has the centre part of its leaves boldly marked with yellow. Of the cultivars of the common ivy, *Hedera helix*, make a special note of 'Buttercup', which is really striking with its golden foliage (this gradually takes on a greenish tinge as the leaves age). Extremely popular, and rightly so, is 'Goldheart' (often misnamed 'Jubilee') with leaves heavily splashed with rich yellow. These and other ivies are remarkably easily pleased, for any ordinary soil suits them and they are not over-fussy about the amount of light they get.

Another delightful wall, fence or trellis plant for a sunny position is the self-supporting *Actinidia kolomikta*, around 10ft (3m) tall and with heart-shaped leaves of a darkish green marked at their lower ends with blotches of white and pink. It introduces a rather exotic flavour into the garden and will grow well given good drainage and a better than average soil. If you have a warm, sunny corner, too, you could also try that tender Chilean climber *Eccremocarpus scaber*, which can be highly decorative during summer with is racemes of red and organge tubular flowers, each about 1in (2.5cm) long. It is best in a lightish soil, for it needs to have good drainage, and you plant it straight from pots in May, after the soil has had a chance to warm up. A climber only for climatically favoured parts of the country, though.

Another climber which can be a wonderful sight on a house

**Opposite:** *The large-flowered clematis cultivar 'Bee's Jubilee' – May-June flowering with more blooms in August.*

Hydrangea petiolaris

wall is the true Virginia creeper, *Parthenocissus quinquefolia*, its pretty, deeply cut leaves turning to glorious shades of scarlet in autumn. It grows well given any aspect. The lovely *P. henryana*, with dark green, silvery-veined foliage, is best on north or west-facing walls. I almost hesitate to mention that rampageous climber the Russian vine, or the mile-a-minute plant. *Polygonum baldschuanicum* certainly deserves that last sobriquet (as it does the first, for it comes from southern Russia) because it is extraordinarily fast growing and will shin up a large wall in next to no time – and smother trees, too, given half a chance. Still, if you want an out-building covered quickly and effectively this is your plant, and the panicles of pinkish-white flowers borne in fluffy clouds in summer and autumn are attractive seen *en masse*. Any well-drained soil will do for this climber. A fine town plant, too, with no sensitivity to traffic-polluted air. I find I appreciate it more and more as time goes by.

The extraordinary adaptability and vigour of the Russian vine is well illustrated by a specimen I know of in a Yorkshire country garden which, although having its roots confined in a quite small container made from the same stone as the wall against which it was built, still covered this wall with the greatest of enthusiasm and very effectively. It was, however, fed lavishly each spring with well-rotted manure from the owner's stable.

A lot of gardeners seem to have no knowledge of the climbing hydrangea, *H. petiolaris*, a self-clinging species (it clings by means of aerial roots), which has its uses in the patio garden if you have an uninviting north-facing wall which you would like to cover to a considerable height. It makes a spreading leafy cover – the leathery leaves are heart-shaped – up to 20ft (6m) tall and as much across, and in June and July bears flat, white flower heads in some profusion.

**Shrubs to grow against walls**
Now just a few more shrubs which, though not climbers, are splendid for growing against walls. First, the pyracanthas, or firethorns, which were so over-planted at one stage that we all got heartily sick of them despite their very real charm. It is a pity, for fine examples like *Pyracantha coccinea* 'Lalandei' will go right up to the house eaves and follow an early summer show of white flowers with a truly brilliant display of orange-red berries in autumn, even in rather shaded positions. So will the rather smaller growing *P. atalantioides* with bright scarlet berries, and *P.* 'Watereri', smaller still, which is especially notable for the freedom with which it bears its red berries. Other free-fruiting varieties are 'Orange Glow' (its orange-red berries are particularly long lasting) and the American-raised 'Mohave'. This last

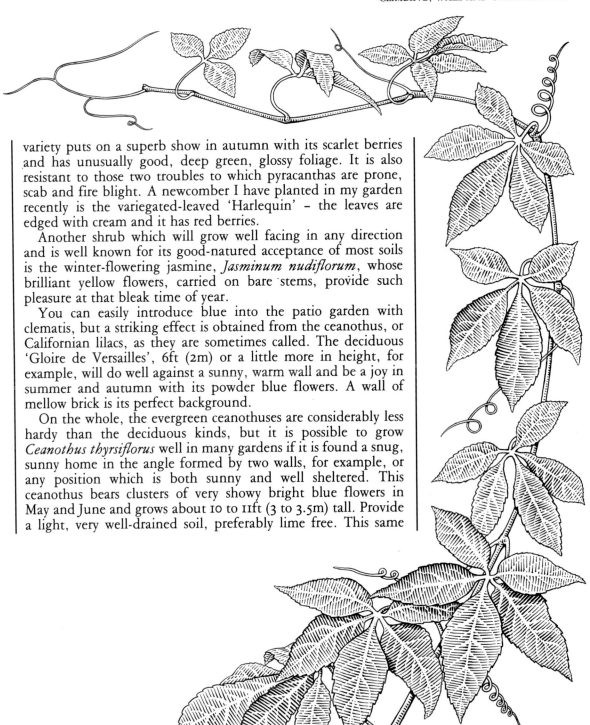

variety puts on a superb show in autumn with its scarlet berries and has unusually good, deep green, glossy foliage. It is also resistant to those two troubles to which pyracanthas are prone, scab and fire blight. A newcomer I have planted in my garden recently is the variegated-leaved 'Harlequin' – the leaves are edged with cream and it has red berries.

Another shrub which will grow well facing in any direction and is well known for its good-natured acceptance of most soils is the winter-flowering jasmine, *Jasminum nudiflorum*, whose brilliant yellow flowers, carried on bare stems, provide such pleasure at that bleak time of year.

You can easily introduce blue into the patio garden with clematis, but a striking effect is obtained from the ceanothus, or Californian lilacs, as they are sometimes called. The deciduous 'Gloire de Versailles', 6ft (2m) or a little more in height, for example, will do well against a sunny, warm wall and be a joy in summer and autumn with its powder blue flowers. A wall of mellow brick is its perfect background.

On the whole, the evergreen ceanothuses are considerably less hardy than the deciduous kinds, but it is possible to grow *Ceanothus thyrsiflorus* well in many gardens if it is found a snug, sunny home in the angle formed by two walls, for example, or any position which is both sunny and well sheltered. This ceanothus bears clusters of very showy bright blue flowers in May and June and grows about 10 to 11ft (3 to 3.5m) tall. Provide a light, very well-drained soil, preferably lime free. This same

Parthenocissus henryana

37

**Opposite:** Hedera helix *'Goldheart', understandably a very popular ivy (see p. 35).*

Ceanothus *'Gloire de Versailles' (see p. 37).*

species, *thrysiflorus*, has a very attractive variety named *repens*, a low-growing and spreading form which goes by the name of creeping blue blossom. It produces its light blue flowers in May with great prodigality and is ideal for growing against a wall facing south or west. It is especially suitable for growing under a downstairs window, for it does not grow more than 4 to 4½ft (1.25 to 1.4m) tall while having a spread of about 6ft (2m).

For growing under a ground-floor window also, or for cover anywhere low down on a wall or fence, there is the herringbone cotoneaster, *C. horizontalis*. The sprays of flat growths are a pleasing sight at any time with their herringbone pattern, but the real beauty comes in autumn when the bright red berries appear in shoals and the leaves turn to rich shades of red before being shed. You can easily keep it to a maximum height of 3ft (1m) although against a wall or other vertical surface it will double this if allowed. An excellent shrub this, too, for a north or east wall, and it will grow in any ordinary soil.

For a sunny position there is the old japonica, correctly *Chaenomeles speciosa*, and its varieties, and the splendid hybrids grouped under the name *C. superba*. In late winter and spring – the actual time of flowering depends on the position of the plant and the weather – the colourful flowers of varieties like the deep red 'Simonii', a useful, low-growing form about 4ft (1.3m) tall and more across, bright orange-scarlet 'Knap Hill Scarlet' and apple-blossom pink and white 'Moerloosei' are a joy. Consider, too, the low-growing 'Pink Lady', a spreading variety only 3ft (1m) or so tall which could be just right for a fence or to grow under a house window. Apart from a need for sunshine, they have no special cultural requirements.

Camellias also provide beautiful blooms early in the year if given wall protection – not an east wall, though, or frost-covered flowers will have their petals 'scorched' by the morning sun. These are mostly varieties of *Camellia japonica*, but they also include some *C. williamsii* hybrids of great beauty. *Camellia japonica* varieties I especially like are 'Adolphe Audusson', with crimson, semi-double blooms, the bright pink 'Elegans' and 'Alba Simplex', white. All camellias, of course, must have a lime-free soil, although if that cannot be arranged in the open garden it is always possible to grow one or two as tub specimens in lime-free compost, with excellent results. Their glossy foliage is an asset throughout the year.

Quite apart from the beauty of the *C. williamsii* hybrids, they have the advantage over the *japonica* varieties of dropping their spent blooms instead of holding on to them and looking rather untidy, unless picked over fairly frequently. The *williamsii* camellias are crosses between *C. japonica* and the more tender *C. saluenensis* and they make very handsome, tallish bushes which are a delight when bearing their flowers in late winter and spring.

The best-known variety is the delectable 'Donation', which has clear pink, semi-double flowers. Others of note include 'J. C. Williams', with pink, single flowers, and 'Francis Hanger' which has white flowers which are also single.

It is always pleasing to grow something a little out of the common run, and if you live in a warmer part of the country do consider finding a home for the pineapple-scented broom, *Cytisus battandieri,* a sizeable deciduous shrub from Morocco which is extremely attractive and is now being much more widely grown than hitherto. It is stocked by numerous leading tree and shrub nurseries.

The soft yellow flowers are borne in upright, cone-shaped clusters in June and July and, as the name suggests, have a pineapple scent. These blooms also have the perfect foil in their grey, silky textured, trifoliate leaves. But you must be prepared for it to grow to a height of 11 to 15ft (3.5 to 4.5) and to have a spread of nearly as much. It is a shrub for the angle formed by two warm walls or a sheltered south or west wall with nearly the protective qualities of the foregoing. Like all brooms, it needs a well-drained soil, preferably rather lean, and as much sunshine as can possibly be provided.

For many years one of my favourite shrubs has been *Garrya elliptica*, a tall-growing evergreen from California which has great decorative value and character. It comes into its own in the second half of winter when it clothes itself with myriad catkins of the most subtle colouring – in some lights silvery-grey, in others more greyish-green – which are borne against a background of oval to roundish, dark green, shiny leaves, greyish on their undersides. What one must be sure to do is get the male form for it is this which has the more impressive catkins, rarely less than 6in (15cm) long but in the most favourable, warm and sheltered conditions almost double that in length.

While *G. elliptica* is hardy as a free-standing shrub in all but cold gardens, it is best to plant it against a wall (for preference facing south or west); and, of course, in the patio garden, where

*Chaenomeles speciosa*
*cultivar (see p. 38).*

space is at a premium, that is what one would wish to do. Against a wall it will reach to a height of 15ft to 20ft (4.5 to 6m). I have associated it with a rambling rose (the American-raised 'Little Compton Creeper', now, alas, no longer offered by nurseries here, at least at the time of writing) and in this way I get the pleasure of the pink flowers of the rose in early summer, its orange hips in autumn and the catkins of the garrya in winter. Perfect! Other climbing roses of the rambler type would associate with it just as well.

Quite fortuitously I planted the garrya quite near to an outside light so that on winter evenings the flick of a switch transforms this lofty shrub into a fairlyland of hanging tassels thrown into bold relief. If you are tempted to give *G. elliptica* a try take note that it must be given a well-drained soil (it need only be of average quality, and it does well on chalk or lime) and that it should be planted young, for it is tricky to transplant although otherwise trouble-free. It is sold as a pot-grown specimen. Arctic winds such as we experience in some winters can brown a proportion of the foliage but I have never known it not overcome such temporary set-backs.

Camellia willamsii
*'Donation'*

Of course, if you have a good expanse of high wall with a warm and sunny aspect going begging and you live in a warmer part of the country, what better to consider growing than that other lovely Californian native, the semi-evergreen *Fremontodendron* 'California Glory', which I mentioned earlier.

This usually grows about 10 to 11ft (3 to 3.5m) tall (although it can be more) and produces an abundance of its golden-yellow, cup-shaped, waxy-textured flowers from late May until July. Again, it is helped by its foliage which is lobed and of dull green colouring and so an attractive foil for the flowers. A rather lean, well-drained soil suits it admirably and it does well on chalky soils.

If this fremontodendron has not proved to be particularly long-lived in gardens here neither has the lovely, deciduous *Abutilon vitifolium* from Chile, but that is no reason to be put off growing either shrub. *A. vitifolium* is a member of the *Malvaceae*, or mallow, family, and is a soft-wooded shrub of great elegance which really needs shelter and warmth such as it will get against a south- or west-facing wall. Given such conditions it will grow to a height of 15 to 20ft (4.5 to 6m) and produce from late May to July (at just the same time as the fremontodendron flowers) an abundance of its distinctive, hollyhock-like, mauve flowers. These also have a splendid foil in the grey, vine-like leaves. The cultivar 'Veronica Tennant' has rather bolder flowers than the species itself and is much in demand for that reason. There is also an attractive white-flowered variety, *album*. These abutilons do well on chalky soils, and indeed on all soils except those of a heavy nature.

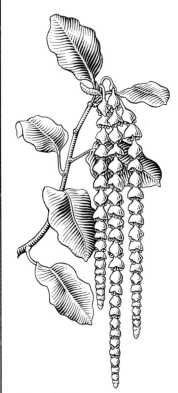

Garrya elliptica

**Opposite:** *Ivies are sympathetic companions for the pretty* Actinidia kolomikta, *the leaves of which are marked with pink and white (see p. 35).*

Its evergreen relative from Brazil, *A. megapotamicum*, is completely different and equally elegant. Growing about 6ft (2m) tall it produces (given the right conditions) a succession of colourful, Chinese-lantern-like flowers from April to autumn on a plant which forms a graceful framework of slender branches clothed with narrow, sharply-pointed leaves of rich green colouring. The pendant flowers with their bright red calyxes, yellow petals and cones of brownish stamens and stigmas are enormously eye-catching. It is a splendid shrub for a warm south- or west-facing wall or for growing in a container. In a bed, it does well in any average soil, provided it is well-drained. There is also a variety with yellow variegated leaves, *A. megapotamicum variegatum* but much as I like variegated-leaved plants generally, in this case I prefer the plain-leaved parent.

Another excellent shrub for growing against a warm, south-facing wall is the evergreen *Choisya ternata*, or Mexican orange blossom. This grows to a height of 8ft (2.5m) or so, has handsome, trifoliate, glossy-surfaced leaves and bears highly fragrant white flowers in terminal clusters in April and May. Flowering sometimes continues intermittently for several months after that. Again, it is a shrub which has no special soil needs, apart from first-class drainage.

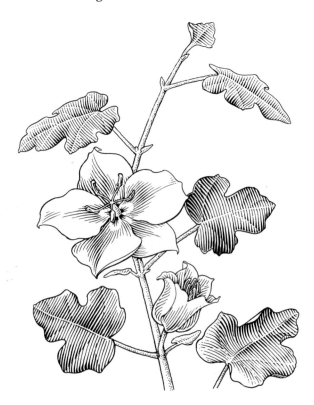

Fremontodendron *'California Glory'* (see p. 41).

Abutilon vitifolium *(see
p. 41)*

### Other shrubs suitable for the patio

Before moving on to other plants I want to mention some other shrubs which would also make a very useful contribution to the patio garden. First, *Senecio* 'Sunshine', the lovely grey-foliaged evergreen shrub beloved of flower arrangers. This will grow 3 to 4ft (1 to 1.3m) tall and as much as 6ft (2m) across, but it is worth the space. What is more, it associates beautifully with a host of other plants, shrubby and perennial. Its silvery-grey leaves age to a soft olive green and are pleasing throughout the year. Sunshine and well-drained soil are all it asks for. The cheerful yellow daisy flowers in June and July can be looked upon as a useful bonus. Quite recently the botanists decided that the plants we have grown for many years in gardens under the names *Senecio greyii* and *S. laxifolius* are, in fact, invariably hybrids between the two and it is these which are now grouped together under the cultivar name 'Sunshine'.

Worth a prominent position and liking light shade is the hybrid mahonia 'Charity' – an evergreen of real value for its rank after rank of spiny leaves – each leaf consisting of up to 21 leaflets – even if one disregards the bold, deep yellow flowers borne in terminal racemes in November and December. You won't be sitting out at that time of year, but how nice to be greeted then by something of such decorative value. It grows something like 10ft (3.5m) tall and 8ft (2.5m) wide (although it can be more), and it is not difficult to please. What it will not tolerate, though, is winter wet at the roots. It can be kept more compact by pruning after flowering in spring. This can, indeed, be most beneficial as it does have a rather stiff habit. The beauty is in those wonderful leaves and flowers.

For spring flowering I would certainly commend the beautiful *Magnolia stellata*, the star magnolia as it is called. This makes a bush perhaps 8ft (2.5m) tall and as much wide, and the pure white star-shaped flowers with their many strap-like petals borne on the bare branches have a special charm. Find it a warm, sunny home where the soil is well-drained and preferably peaty. It is best without lime. Unlike most magnolias, it starts to flower at an early age.

If, on grounds of size, the easily pleased and very attractive *M. soulangiana* must be ruled out by most patio-garden owners, then there is another large magnolia which can be considered – the magnificent *M. grandiflora*, which is not all that hardy and so is invariably grown against a south- or south-west-facing wall. But it must be a high wall for it can, in time, reach a height of 26ft (8m), although it may well stick at something less. It also needs good

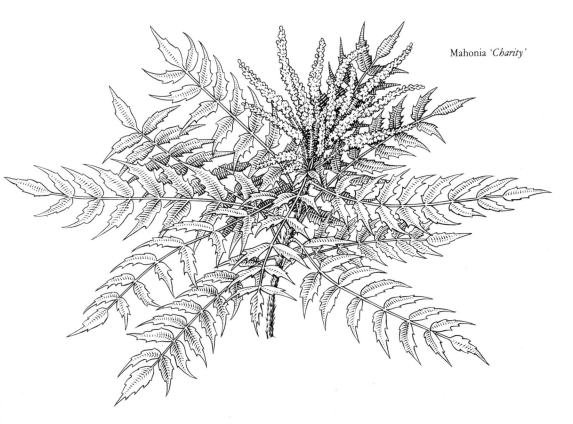

Mahonia *'Charity'*

45

**Opposite:** Pyracantha
*'Orange Glow', which fruits
over a long period and is a
favourite with many gardeners.*
*(see p. 36)*

soil. What a job it is, though, when carrying its imposing creamy-white, fragrant, bowl-shaped flowers from July to September. The ovate leaves are dark green and glossy, and covered on the underside with a reddish-brown felt, as its most pronounced on young foliage. It is lime-tolerant. 'Exmouth' is a fine cultivar.

I would always try to find a home for *Paeonia lutea ludlowii* for this is a tree paeony of outstanding beauty from spring to autumn although I have to admit that it has a rather gaunt appearance in winter. It grows about 5ft (1.5m) tall and wide and is a delight when bearing the bold, deeply cut, fresh green leaves. Its peak period for effectiveness, though, is in May and June when for about three weeks these leaves form the frame for its superb rich golden-yellow, single flowers of cup-like appearance. Again, like the magnolias just referred to, this shrub needs sunshine, shelter and good soil drainage. In the patio garden even more than larger gardens it is an asset to have at least one or two different plants with very obvious "architectural" qualities (using that term in its gardening sense), for shape can be just as pleasing to the eye as beauty of flower, berry or foliage.

A shrub which associates splendidly with paving is the colourful *Hypericum* 'Hidcote', and given a well-drained soil it will flourish in sunshine or light shade. What a sight it is, too, when its rounded frame is smothered from early August until late September with the golden-yellow, saucer-like flowers – a mound of colour 4ft (1.3m) or so tall and perhaps 6ft (2m) wide.

Consider growing, too, a few potentillas, or cinquefoils as they are called, for those, mostly yellow-flowered but with some cream and white and the odd one having orange, red or pink blooms are quite low-growing – anything from 1ft to 4ft (30cm to 1.3m) tall and 3ft to 5ft (1m to 1.5m) wide, depending on cultivar – and provide colour the summer through from June to September or even October. Both the single flowers and the leaves are small and borne in profusion. Especially valuable is the cultivar 'Goldfinger', 3ft (90cm) tall, which is another of those

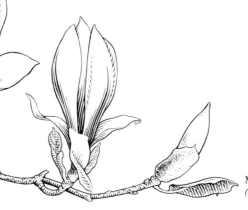

Magnolia soulangiana
*(see p. 45).*

shrubs with bright gold-yellow flowers to bring gaiety to the garden scene.

Other splendid potentiallas are 'Primrose Beauty', a lovely combination of colours with its primrose-yellow flowers and greyish-green foliage. This makes a spreading bush some 4ft (1.3m) tall and up to 6ft (2m) wide. But there are many more to choose from. 'Red Ace' is vermilion-flame, a strong colour which fades in very hot, dry weather and in very wet conditions. 'Royal Flush', with single rose-pink flowers, is highly attractive, 1ft (30cm) tall and 2ft (60cm) wide. 'Princess' has soft pink flowers and is 2½ft (75cm) tall and wide. All shrubby potentillas are extremely accommodating about soil conditions, and, although liking sunshine, they do well in light shade.

The admirable *Syringa meyeri* 'Palibin' (syn. *S. palibiniana, S. velutina*), not at all that well-known, is a natural choice for the patio garden – only 4ft (1.3m) tall and wide and with the most attractive rounded leaves, perfectly in scale, and fragrant, rosy-lilac flowers in May. Also, for the front of the border where its growth can splay over the paving, there is a delightful dwarf broom in *Cytisus kewensis*, only 1ft (30cm) tall but up to 5ft (1.5m) across, which bears sulphur-yellow flowers from late April to late May. Good soil drainage is an absolute necessity for this lime-tolerant shrub.

A dome-shaped shrub about 3ft (1m) tall which is very colourful in late May and June is *Genista hispanica*, the Spanish gorse. It smothers itself then with its bright golden-yellow pea flowers. Intensely prickly and much branched, it forms an impenetrable mass and as this network of spines and branches stays a rich green in winter it has an evergreen appearance although deciduous. What you must provide it with is a position in full sun where the soil is well drained. It will not tolerate excessive winter wet.

A dwarf cherry of great value for the patio garden is *Prunus glandulosa* 'Albiplena', another of those shrubs which although long grown in this country is not at all well-known. It grows only 3 to 4ft (1 to 1.3m) tall and wide and bears its double white flowers prolifically in late April and early May. Then in the autumn the leaves take on the most lovely tawny-red shade, sometimes suffused with lilac. It has a pink-flowered counterpart in *P. glandulosa* 'Sinensis'. A good loamy soil is appreciated by both these cherries, but whatever the composition of the soil it must be well drained – something which has to be stressed with so many shrubs. It is worth noting, too, that these cherries, like others of their kind, grow well on chalky soils.

Another prunus, which should be considered is the dwarf almond *P. tenella* 'Fire Hill', which makes a lovely show in April when the upright branches are smothered in rosy-red flowers. This is also a small shrub, 3 to 4ft (1 to 1.3m) tall and more wide.

Do not overlook either the lovely small-growing laurel, *P. laurocerasus* 'Otto Luyken', which I have described in the chapter on plants for containers (p. 120).

I shall not say much about hydrangeas, superb as these are for the patio garden, for I also deal with them in the chapter on plants to grow in containers (see p. 117), but one I must mention – the comparative newcomer *Hydrangea* 'Preziosa'. This hybrid, which has the common hydrangea, *H. macrophylla*, as one parent and *H. serrata* as the other, makes a bush at most 5ft (1.5m) tall and 4ft (1.3m) wide and usually rather less, so although showy it does not take up too much space. Its pride and joy are the round, hortensia-type (mop-headed) blooms in salmon-pink, usually borne with much freedom, and with these are combined foliage and stems tinted with purple – a delightful combination of colours. This shrub is a fine choice for any but dry soils (which all hydrangeas loathe, of course) and it is happy in sunshine or light shade.

Grow *Daphne mezereum* if you can find room, in sunshine or light shade in a rather good, moisture-retentive but well-drained soil, for the very fragrant purplish-red flowers which bedeck its bare, upright 4 to 5ft (1.3 to 1.5m) frame in February and March are a special treat. Accept, however, that this deciduous shrub can die on you for no apparent reason while still reasonably young.

Another daphne which it is well worth finding a home for is the 4 to 5ft (1.3 to 1.5m) tall *D. odora* 'Aureomarginata', an evergreen which produces in late winter and early spring richly scented small flowers in terminal heads. These flowers are near white within and purplish-red on the outside of the petals. The shiny, oval leaves are of mid-green colouring and are margined with creamy-white. Although this variety is hardier than the species itself it still needs a sheltered position, but that shouldn't be difficult to find in your patio garden. Culturally, its needs are similar to those of *D. mezereum*. There will surely be a real place in the future, too, for *D. bholua* 'Gurkha', a 7 to 8ft (2.25 to 2.5m) deciduous shrub from the Himalayas, which bears purplish-rose flowers of strong fragrance between December and February. It is upright in habit.

To grow rhododendrons and azaleas you must have a lime-free humusy soil which is retentive of moisture, but given this it can be very well worthwhile incorporating in the garden just the odd one or two of the smaller-flowering rhododendrons. I'm thinking particularly of things like the slow-growing *R. yakushimanum*, an outstanding Japanese species which grows 4ft (1.3m) tall and wide at most and has lovely bell-shaped blooms which are pink in the bud and open white. It is May-flowering.

A group of compact hybrids of small stature has been developed from this species, these being of considerable interest

Rhododendron
yakushimanum

49

to the gardener lacking space. They have a good colour range and superb kinds include 'Morning Magic' with white flowers which are pink in the bud; 'Hydon Hunter', with pink flowers, edged with red and with orange spotting; and 'Caroline Allbrook' a lavender colour. 'Diana Pearson', a very attractive blush pink with crimson spotting was, I am delighted to say, named for my wife by Mr Arthur George, the rhododendron breeder who has had remarkable success with his 'Yak' hybrids. Other rhododen-

Rhododendron yakushiamanum *hybrids, like 'Caroline Allbrook' shown here, are ideal for growing on patios – of course, in lime-free soil.*

drons worth your consideration – and there are, of course, many more from which to make a choice – are the lavender-blue 'Blue Diamond', which has the most becoming small leaves, and the dark red 'Elizabeth', which makes a spreading bush not more than 4ft (1.3m) tall, or about the same as the much more compact 'Blue Diamond'. Both are April flowering.

Then there is the highly attractive 'Bow Bells' which bears bell-shaped flowers of an exquisite shade of soft pink in April and

Rhus typhina

May. It also has very attractive rounded, heart-shaped leaves, which it inherits from the *R. williamsianum* side of its parentage. It grows about 3ft (1m) tall and has a spreading habit. A hybrid which I have loved ever since I first saw it at the Chelsea Flower Show where it won an award of merit is 'Pink Pebble', a small, shapely bush with rounded leaves (from the *williamsianum* side of its parentage) and exquisite pale pink bell flowers in May which open from bright red buds.

For earlier, March, flowering a couple of small-growing rhododendron hybrids I would especially commend to attention are 'Seta' and 'Tessa Roza'. The first is an especially attractive, rather upright-growing variety up to 4ft (1.3m) tall which bears tubular bell flowers of near white colouring striped with pink; 'Tessa Roza', up to 5ft (1.5m) tall, had rose-pink flowers which are especially good for cutting for indoor decoration – if you can bring yourself to remove even a few sprigs for that purpose. Both have a common parent in *R. moupinense* which has passed on to them an ability to withstand drought conditions better than most rhododendrons. Because they flower so early in the year there is a risk of frost damage to the blooms although the plants themselves are fully hardy. For this reason it is best to avoid planting them in positions where the blooms will be exposed to early morning sunshine and damage through ''scorching''.

For late May colour a specimen or two of Knap Hill and Exbury hybrid deciduous azaleas could be good value, especially as the leaves often colour up well in autumn, while of the evergreen azaleas I would put in a word for the exquisite white-flowered 'Palestrina' and 'Vuyk's Rosy Red'. Again, these are May flowering, little over 4ft (1.3m) tall and 4 to 5ft (1.3 to 1.5m) across.

The stag's horn sumach, *Rhus typhina,* has a rather angular appearance and gets quite large – as much as 13 to 15ft (4 to 4.5m) tall and as much across, a low-branching tree more than a shrub, perhaps – and throws up suckers which can be a bit of a nuisance, but I still consider it very worthwhile for a sunny corner of a patio garden, at least one which is not too small. The large pinnate leaves, sometimes more than 2ft (60cm) long, are most attractive and colour beautifully in autumn – a variety of shades from red and orange to yellow and purple – and female specimens too offer another attraction in their crimson, cone-shaped fruit clusters which appear late in the year. Greenish-coloured flower panicles are borne by specimens of both sexes in July. It has no special soil needs. A cut-leaved female form named 'Laciniata' is also available and can be a source of pleasure in the garden.

A rather sprawly shrub from the Mediterranean region which is especially well-suited for patio conditions is the Jerusalem sage, *Phlomis fruticosa,* an evergreen with grey-green, sage-like leaves and pretty yellow flowers which are borne in whorls on the upper parts of the stems in early summer. About 4ft (1.3m) tall, it is a lovely sight spreading out, in its uninhibited way, over the edge of a bed on to paving. This is another of those shrubs which must be given a warm, sunny position, and it is best in rather lean soil, which must be well-drained.

Indeed, those are just the conditions to suit the rock roses I mentioned earlier (*Cistus skanbergii* [see p. 23] and a selection of hybrids of which the best is probably 'Silver Pink', up to 3ft [1m] tall and wide and very beautiful in the first half of summer when the silvery-pink flowers are borne in quantity against a background of dark green leaves). These evergreens are worth a bit of pampering. They establish best from spring planting, and love sunshine combined with shelter. Indeed, they are often known as sun roses rather than rock roses. In very severe winter weather it is a wise precaution to protect them as far as possible with dry litter.

One does not want to overdo such effects but a few really good variegated shrubs can be stunningly effective in a small garden. Two in particular I would bring to your attention: *Weigela florida variegata* and *Elaeagnus pungens* 'Maculata'. The weigela is deciduous, the elaeagnus evergreen. The first has a height and spread of 4 to 5ft (1.3 to 1.5m), the second makes a rather bigger bush. Both are happy in any reasonable, well-drained soil. The decorative value of the weigela is at its peak in early summer when the creamy-white-edged leaves make a marvellous foil for the pink, foxglove-like flowers, but the foliage alone is a decorative feature right up to leaf fall. The elaeagnus stands on the decorative value of its foliage alone, and that it does splendidly. The leaves with their rich mixture of green and gold positively glow in sunshine the year round, and they brighten the garden even in the dullest of weather.

One must always allow for the ubiquitous but invaluable forsythia to make a bush 7 to 10ft (2.3 to 3m) tall, but do find a nice corner site for it, in sunshine or shade – it will do well in either. The best known and most widely planted is the excellent *Forsythia intermedia spectabilis,* and a splendid sight it is in March and April, but even better is another variety belonging to the same *intermedia* grouping – 'Lynwood' which bears masses of large, rich yellow blooms. More upright-growing is 'Beatrix Farrand', an American-raised variety which has extra-large flowers of golden-yellow. I find it less free-flowering than the other two just mentioned.

If you are, for instance, making a feature of a birch tree (see the chapter on trees, p. 69) then you might care to give this an extra bit of sparkle by planting a few heathers around its base. Most heathers demand a lime-free soil, but an important group of winter-flowering ericas (*Erica carnea* and its numerous varieties) are among those tolerant of lime, and it is those I have in mind

*Rhododendrons provide a telling backdrop to this paved area.*

now to bring additional colour to the garden in the winter.

These *Erica carnea* varieties come in heights up to about 15in (38cm) so are enormously useful for providing a low carpet of colour. Two strong-growing, spreading varieties are 'Springwood White' and 'Springwood 'Pink', these flowering freely from January to March or April. Others of note are the deep red, bronze-foliaged 'Vivelli' (February-March flowering); 'Myretoun Ruby', with ruby-red flowers from February to April; the ground-

**Below:** Rhododendron yakushimanum *'Hydon Hunter', one of a group of hybrids of compact habit ideal for patio gardens (see p. 50).*

hugging, golden-foliaged 'Foxhollow' with pink flowers during the same period; and the vigorous 'Pink Spangles', which flowers from January to March. There are plenty of others to choose from. It is always a good thing to add plenty of peat to the soil in which heathers are to be grown, and make sure that they do not suffer from undue dryness at the roots, especially during the establishment period.

For providing low cover in less than ideal conditions I would always turn to the adaptable periwinkles or vincas, and particularly *Vinca major* 'Variegata (often known also as *V. major* 'Elegantissima'). This bears pretty purplish-blue flowers from April to June, and is attractive the year round as a foliage plant for the evergreen leaves are heavily marked with creamy-white. It grows about 1ft (30cm) tall and has a spread of about 3ft (1m).

I mentioned two hebes at the beginning of this chapter which give excellent value, 'Great Orme' and 'Autumn Glory'. The first makes a shrub some 3 to 4ft (1 to 1.3m) tall and wide, the second, one which is 2ft (60cm) tall and around 3ft (1m) wide. 'Great Orme' bears longish spikes of pink flowers from early summer to July; 'Autumn Glory' much shorter spikes of violet-blue flowers from July into autumn, so they complement each other very well indeed. Like all the hebes they do well in any well-drained soil of average quality in a sunny position.

Two low-growing, ground-covering hebes which are also very useful for patio-garden planting are 'Carl Teschner', which bears short spikes of violet-coloured flowers in mid-summer against a background of dark green leaves, and *H. pinguifolia* 'Pagei' which has a mass of glaucous-grey leaves and bears clusters of small white flowers in May. This last in particular has become very popular as a ground-coverer in recent years. Both of these plants grow about 9in to 1ft (23cm to 30cm) tall and have a spread of about 3ft (1m). *H. pinguifolia* 'Pagei' makes a lovely plant to associate with the very attractive herbaceous geranium, *G. sanguineum lancastriense,* which has pale pink flowers with red veining. This geranium flowers practically all summer.

One of the best evergreen ground-cover shrubs, not more than 1ft (30cm) tall, is the popular and eye-catching *Euonymus fortunei* 'Emerald 'n' Gold', the leaves of which are bright yellow and green and often tinged with pink. It is suitable for growing in sunshine or light shade and in any reasonable soil.

Shrubs which provide strong garden features in their own right and at the same time make splendid foils for other border plants are always to be welcomed, and *Berberis thunbergii atropurpurea* falls squarely in that category. This deciduous barberry grows about 5 to 6ft (1.5 to 2m) tall and wide and has small reddish-purple leaves which are set off by small yellow flowers in spring. Then, at the other end of the season, the leaves intensify in colour before leaf fall. This variety has a dwarf form 'Atropurpurea Nana', no more than 2ft (60cm) tall, which is a fine plant to provide special effects where space is limited, as in raised beds. Although very easy-going, like all the barberries, neither *atropurpurea* nor its dwarf form are happy in chalk soils.

Another variety of *B. thunbergii* which is admirably suited to the patio garden is 'Rose Glow', some 5ft (1.5m) tall and wide which has purple leaves mottled with silvery-pink and rose while these are at the young stage (later they become purple all over).

For a sunny position where the soil is well drained I commend also the attractive, compact form of the deciduous *Physocarpus opulifoius* named 'Dart's Gold', which grows some 2½ft to 3ft (75cm to 1m) tall and wide. From spring onwards its three- or five-lobed leaves are a rich golden-yellow, which does however take on some greenish overtones as summer advances. It bears white flowers in June, but it is the foliage which counts.

Another true dwarf form of a popular barberry is *B. stenophylla* 'Coronilla Compacta' – a frightful mouthful of a name for an attractive little 1½ft (45cm) tall shrub which bears yellow flowers in April which are coral-red in the bud stage. It's another candidate for a raised bed.

There is one other barberry to which I would give brief mention: 'Parkjuweel', a very prickly, semi-evergreen variety which is noted for its fine autumn leaf colouring. It bears yellow flowers in spring and makes a compact bush some 4ft (1.3m) tall and 2½ft (75cm) across.

Skimmia japonica
*'Foremanii'*

For special autumnal effects don't overlook either that splendid cotoneaster, *C. conspicuus* 'Decorus', which grows some 3ft (1m) tall and more wide and smothers itself in small bright red berries during early autumn, these persisting well into winter. Then there is the low-growing *C. dammeri,* only a few inches high but with a spread of 2 to 3ft (60cm to 1m), which is an excellent ground-coverer and free in the production of its small red berries in autumn. Both can be grown in any average soil, preferably in a sunny position but in light shade if need be.

For warm, sunny positions and well-drained soils a good choice where something low-growing is required is the lavender, *Lavandula angustifolia* 'Hidcote', 2ft (60cm) tall and with spikes of violet-blue flowers in the second half of summer. If something taller is needed then a good choice would be the rosemary, *Rosmarinus officinalis* 'Fastigiatus', which is also known as 'Miss Jessop's Variety'. This grows 5 to 6ft (1.5 to 2m) tall and bears blue flowers in May and intermittently during summer.

Some of the smaller-growing forms of the Japanese maple, *Acer palmatum,* are delightful patio shrubs with their attractive shapes and foliage. Two of the most suitable are *A. palmatum* 'Dissectum' and *A. palmatum* 'Dissectum Atropurpureum' for they have deeply cut foliage, this of a fetching fresh green colour in the first case and bronze-purple in the other. In both the leaves colour well before leaf-fall, assuming red shades. These *A. palmatum* cultivars are not, however, suitable for chalky soils.

For a shady spot a splendid shrub of smallish stature is *Skimmia japonica* 'Foremanii', an evergreen with glossy leaves which grows 3ft (1m) and up to 6ft (2m) wide. It bears conspicuous red berries from autumn right through the winter but only if you plant it near a male variety of *S. japonica* 'Fragrans', for skimmia is a genus in which the sexes are divided. Both varieties bear

**Above:** Euonymus fortunei *'Emerald 'n' Gold'*, a first-class, low-growing evergreen ground-cover shrub.

**Opposite:** Euonymus fortunei *'Silver Queen'* associated with Hosta sieboldiana *and* Polygonatum x hybridum (Solomon's seal) to create a beautiful "mural corner".

white flowers in spring, those of 'Fragrans' being nicely scented, as the name suggests. *S. japonica* 'Rubella' is attractive for it bears red buds in winter which open to white flowers in April.

Another small shrub of value, but this time for a sunny position, is *Spiraea bumalda* 'Anthony Waterer', some 3ft (1m) tall and wide, with panicles of bright red flowers through most of summer set off by lance-shaped leaves of dark green, often flecked pink and cream. Any average soil suits it well. Another, no more than 2ft (60cm) high, and very free-flowering, is

Fuchsia *'Mrs Popple'*

*S, japonica* 'Alpina' which bears a profusion of rose-pink flowers in summer. This does well in light shade. Another I am very fond of is *S. nipponica tosaensis* (more often known as 'Snowmound') which literally does become a 4 to 5ft (1.25 to 1.50m) mound of white when it flowers in June.

Three viburnums must also be given special mention: the evergreen *V. davidii*, some 2 to 3ft (60cm to 1m) tall and as much across, *V. tinus* 'Eve Price', 6ft (2m) tall and perhaps a little more wide and *V. tinus* 'Gwenllian'. *V. davidii* has very attractive, deeply veined leaves of dark green colouring and, on female specimens (for this again is a shrub where the sexes are separated and you need to plant male and female forms to get berries), turquoise-blue berries in winter, while the compact-growing form of the popular evergreen laurustinus, *V. tinus* 'Eve Price', bears through most of the winter heads of pale pink flowers which are carmine-coloured in the bud. It is worth a prominent position. Compact-growing *V. tinus* 'Gwenllian' produces blue berries freely and is a lovely sight with these among the pink flowers. These, and indeed all, viburnums like a soil of reasonably good quality which is moisture-retentive but well drained. They should also be planted in positions open to plenty of sunshine.

I have more to say about fuchsias in the chapter on plants for containers (see p. 117) and there is no doubting the usefulness of the hardiest of these for planting permanently in sheltered borders. They include *Fuchsia magellanica* 'Versicolor' (which makes a bush of spreading habit up to 5ft [1.5m] tall) and the hardiest of the many hybrids which are available. This is a spectacular shrub with its grey-green leaves marked with creamy-white and pink and its red and violet flowers in summer (it is, however, primarily a foliage shrub), but like the other kinds referred to above it can be cut right back in severe winters. New growth breaks freely from the base in spring, however, although you should take the precaution of protecting the roots in winter with a covering of dry litter or well-weathered ashes. Winter wet is also a natural hazard, and you should make sure that the soil is free-draining by working in plenty of humus-forming material like garden compost or peat.

A few of the numerous varieties suitable for planting in this way are 'Mrs Popple', with scarlet and purple flowers; 'Margaret', crimson and violet-purple, semi-double; 'Alice Hoffman', cerise and white; 'Chillerton Beauty', white, pink and violet-mauve; and 'Tom Thumb', cerise and mauve, a popular dwarf variety. These and others will provide a mass of colour right through from mid-summer to autumn, especially in lightly shaded parts of the garden.

Don't overlook the charm of such bamboos as *Arundinaria murieliae,* the variegated *A. viridistriata* and the small 'Gauntletii'.

*Only glass separates this extension to an existing house from the patio garden measuring 23ft (7m) across by 28ft (8.6m) long. To help preserve a sense of space 1ft (30cm) square tiles are used instead of larger paving slabs. The weeping birch,* Betula pendula youngii, *is never likely to be a nuisance because of size.*

*At the farther end of the garden 10ft (3m) square of ground is screened by runner beans and the space in between is used to grow a few vegetables and fruit on the walls. As it is so close to the house, the support for the beans is made tidy by having a sawn-timber frame with bamboo canes or cord actually*

*providing the support for the plants.*

*Two wide steps drop down beside a small pool fed by a fountain. This is sited exactly opposite a seat built into the wall on the left. It is an easily maintained garden which should give quiet satisfaction throughout the year.*

The first forms a clump up to 10ft (3m) tall with arching stems which start green and later take on a yellow tinge. The 6ft (2m) *A. viridistriata* has leaves striped with yellow and purplish-green canes, while *A.* 'Gauntletii' is of only half this height and has canes which turn from a rich green to a purplish shade. These can look extremely attractive in a paved setting.

The best time of all to plant these is in April and May but October is another good planting month. Provide them with a home in a sheltered position in good soil which does not dry out.

Perhaps rather surprisingly, I am going to suggest that you also consider finding a home for that favourite of the Victorians,

**Opposite:** Arundinaria viridistriata, *one of the most striking of the variegated bamboos (see p. 61)*

the evergreen shrub which also doubles up as a striking house plant – *Fatsia japonica.* You will probably know it for its large, deeply lobed, shiny leaves of darkest green, perhaps less well for the panicles of rather handsome white flowers which appear in late autumn. In the garden it has value as an architectural plant – that is to say, one with beauty of form. In really cold gardens it will have to have the protection of a warm wall, but elsewhere any reasonably sheltered spot will suffice, and that should include most patio gardens.

**Pruning shrubs**

Earlier in this chapter I outlined the pruning treatment which clematis need for these are, as the saying goes, a rather special case. Now I want to give a few tips on the pruning of shrubs in general which I hope you will find useful when you come to wield your secateurs.

I would urge above all a modicum of restraint. Do what is necessary, but always be conscious that what you have removed has taken a long time to develop and cannot be put back.

As with rose pruning, the way to an easy mind is to have a basic understanding of the underlying principles, and it is these which I shall discuss now.

With shrubs one is pruning for shapeliness, good health (by removing dead and weak wood) and vigour. I shall at this stage divide shrubs into two sections – the deciduous and the evergreen, the latter needing little in the way of pruning attention.

Deciduous shrubs are again sub-divided into those which flower on wood made in the same year and those which flower on the previous season's wood. All the earlier flowering shrubs fall in the latter category, and these can again be split into those which flower before growth starts in spring and those which start to flower either coincidentally with the start of growth or rather later in the season.

The first category, the early flowerers, like the forsythias, you should prune as soon as flowering has finished, so that all the growth which follows will be left to bear flowers in the following year. If this job is done later in the year, after growth has been made, then obviously good potential flowering wood must be cut away – and there is no gain in that.

Those shrubs which flower at or after the start of growth in spring are still pruned immediately after flowering finishes but it is done in the knowledge that inevitably some potential new flowering wood must be lost. You therefore prune with some circumspection, only cutting away wood which you feel must go for the overall good of the plant.

Shrubs which flower in late summer on the wood made in the same year are easy to deal with: you can prune these at any time during winter until growth restarts in spring.

*When discussing patios the natural inclination is to think of houses or properties with a rather contemporary air, but of course many small plots accompany period terraced houses. With these, it is important that care should be taken to make the paved sitting-out area and plantings completely in character. This plot represents an area 42ft (12.6m) wide by 60ft (18m) deep and the design allows for ample sitting-out space near the building. Then there is a drop of 15in (38cm) to what could either be a small lawn or another paved area, according to taste, with or without the pool at the centre. If it were decided not to have a pool then a bowl, sundial or similar ornament set in a grouping of low-growing plants would be an admirable alternative.*

*Even a garden of this size can have its compost corner if this is screened from the house, as here by a carefully executed trellis screen.*

With evergreens, confine the pruning to the removal of dead or weak wood and a bit of shaping up – and do this in spring when the plants have a time of strong growth ahead of them. One other thing you can do though with evergreens, if need be, is to invigorate old specimens by shortening the branches quite severely in early spring. Such treatment will encourage strong new growth to be made.

As to the execution, always use sharp secateurs or pruners and make the cuts close to a joint on the stem so that there will be no risk of die-back. Dispose of all prunings immediately to avoid the risk of decay and the spread of diseases.

# 4. A Small Tree for Atmosphere

Like most people I reserve a special place in my affections for trees. They do something for gardens and the landscape generally which is of inestimable value, and many of these have such character that they seem almost to have personalities of their own.

When considering trees in relation to the patio garden, though, it is necessary to curb one's enthusiasm and make quite sure that their dimensions are suitable for such a setting. There is nothing more distressing than to see some beautiful tree cut back, even mutilated, because there is insufficient room for it to develop as it should. So check first what the ultimate size of any tree you are considering is likely to be. It will vary with the conditions, of course, but it is possible to arrive at a rough mean which is a good enough guide.

What I have said about planting shrubs and their aftercare (see pp. 24 to 25) applies with equal force to trees, so I will not repeat it here. Be quite sure to provide adequate support, for if there is anything which is going to set back the re-establishment of a newly planted tree it is wind rocking, which does not give the questing roots a chance to gain a firm hold. And be sure to place the stake in position before setting the tree in the prepared hole. Doing this afterwards can easily cause severe damage to the roots.

What are the qualities to look for when choosing a tree for a patio setting? Well, it goes without saying that it must be of modest or reasonable size. Its form must be pleasing and right for the surroundings. Indeed, I think this can often be more important than the consideration of such transient pleasures as beauty of flower, berry or foliage (except in the case of evergreens). With flowering trees, and there are some delightful small ones, you must consider whether their colouring will fit in with that of other plants you expect to have in bloom at the same time. In a larger garden this is something which one need scarcely bother about, but in the confines of a small area, where everything is closely related, it is a factor to consider.

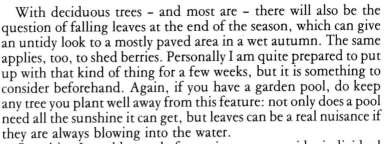

With deciduous trees – and most are – there will also be the question of falling leaves at the end of the season, which can give an untidy look to a mostly paved area in a wet autumn. The same applies, too, to shed berries. Personally I am quite prepared to put up with that kind of thing for a few weeks, but it is something to consider beforehand. Again, if you have a garden pool, do keep any tree you plant well away from this feature: not only does a pool need all the sunshine it can get, but leaves can be a real nuisance if they are always blowing into the water.

One thing I would stress before going on to consider individual trees for the patio is the action necessary if you want to remove a branch from a mature tree because it has died, is diseased or is, perhaps, just badly placed and so spoiling the symmetry of its outline.

The danger here is that when the branch is semi-severed its weight will bring it down and cause a tear in the bark which will take long to heal. You can easily stop this happening by making an undercut first. With heavy branches – anything you cannot support with your free hand – it is always wise to do the job in two stages: make the first cut about 2ft (60cm) from the trunk and finally saw it off flush with the trunk after the branch is out of the way. Then pare the edges of the wound smooth with a pruning knife and cover the whole area with a bituminous sealing agent to protect it from the weather and the entry of diseases. You can get tree wound dressings of this kind at garden stores, and they are easily painted on the wounds.

**Prunus and Malus**

Now for a few planting suggestions. The genus *Prunus* includes all the flowering cherries, peaches, almonds, plums and the ubiquitous and useful laurels and offers infinite delights to gardeners of all persuasions. A splendid choice for the patio would be the pyramidal *Prunus* 'Amanogawa' which makes a slim column 15 to 20ft (4.5 to 6m) tall and smothers itself in late April and May with shell-pink blooms. Similar, but perhaps 5ft (1.5m) taller, is *P. hillieri* 'Spire', with a maximum width of about 10ft (3m), which bears soft pink flowers and provides a bonus in having good autumn colour.

For the rather more generously sized patio. I would certainly suggest the lovely flowering plum *P. blireana* as an alternative. It makes a beautifully rounded small tree, perhaps 18 to 20ft (5.5 to 6m) tall and about as wide, with double, rose-pink blooms in

Prunus '*Amanogawa*'

**Opposite:** Malus '*John Downie*', *an ornamental crab of excellence.*

Prunus *'Kiku Shidare Sakura'*

April. The coppery-bronze foliage is also an attraction from spring to autumn. One cautionary note, though: the colours of most bricks clash with the blooms, so try to avoid such a juxtaposition. It is best of all with a dark background, such as in a larger garden could easily be provided by a conifer screen.

The modestly-sized winter-flowering cherry, *P. subhirtella* 'Autumnalis', is also worth considering if colour at that time of year interests you, for it produces its white, semi-double blooms intermittently right through from late autumn until March.

The Fuji cherry, *P. incisa,* is grown either as a shrub or a small tree, and in both roles it is a sheer delight, smothering itself, as winter gives way to spring, with white flowers which are pink at the bud stage. Its heavily toothed leaves usually also colour up well before leaf fall. It does not often grow much more than 15ft (4.5m). tall

A Japanese cherry to consider is the round-headed and late-flowering 'Shimidsu Sakura', another charmer, which again grows only some 15 to 18ft (4.5 to 5.5m) tall and wide. The branches droop over prettily to create a beautiful effect when it is in flower, these flowers being semi-double, pinkish in the bud stage and opening pure white. They appear in May. Even smaller in stature and a little earlier flowering (late April and early May) is the weeping 'Kiku Shidare Sakura' which bears fully double, deep pink flowers to make it the ideal weeping tree for patio-garden conditions. It can look stunning underplanted with the grape hyacinth, *Muscari armeniacum* 'Heavenly Blue', which is in flower at the same time.

Any ordinary soil suits these cherries and they like lime. They need sunshine and good drainage.

A reasonable soil, good drainage and exposure to all the sunshine that is going is what is needed, too, by pretty ornamental crabs like *Malus* 'Golden Hornet'. This particular cultivar makes a tree of 20 to 26ft (6 to 8m) or so in height and much the same spread, and it is lovely in spring when covered in white blossom and again in autumn and winter when the long-persisting bright yellow fruits cover the branches. 'John Downie', of similar size, is another, this having pleasing yellow and red fruits.

Roughly the same size is the Japanese crab, *M. floribunda,* a spectacular sight in late April when it smothers itself with pale pink, single flowers, red at the bud stage. Yellow fruits follow in autumn. An ornamental crab of columnar habit which can also be a good choice is the variety 'Van Eseltine' which has rosy-pink, double flowers, red at the bud stage.

My favourite of them all, though, is *Malus* x *robusta* 'Yellow Siberian' which makes a small tree of great charm. It bears white flowers (sometimes flushed with pink) in April and a profusion of small yellow fruits in autumn, these being long-persisting. In flower and fruit it is a joy.

*Betula pendula youngii*

## Elegant form and decorative bark

I am fond, too, of the weeping birch, *Betula pendula youngii*, so elegant at all times and not difficult to accommodate as it grows only some 15 to 20ft (4.5 to 6m) tall. It also relates most sympathetically to other garden features. Although taller (up to 40ft [12m]) the related Swedish birch, *B. p. dalecarlica*, whose pendulous branches carry the loveliest of finely cut leaves, does not have a great lateral spread and its natural elegance makes it worth considering for larger patios. All birches are rather greedy feeders, although they will put up with very lean fare when occasion demands. They will do best, though, in soils with plenty of body. There is much pleasure to be gained also from the yellow leaf tints which these and other birches assume in autumn. It will be up to you to decide whether their visual appeal justifies putting up with the disadvantages referred to, in a patio garden.

A choice maple to grow if you can provide a sunny, sheltered home and well-drained soil is *Acer griseum*, a species with beautiful flaking bark and good autumn colour. It does not usually grow over 20ft (6m) tall and 10ft (3m) wide. Much the same size is *A. ginnala* with most spectacular autumn colouring in deep orange and red. This you can grow as a small tree or large shrub.

**Opposite:** Sorbus
hupehensis, *an elegant small
tree which bears long-lasting
fruits (see p. 72).*

**Right:** Sorbus *'Joseph Rock'
- one of the finest of the
mountain ashes.*

Quite different again are the snake-bark maples of which the
small-growing *A. pensylvanicum* is an example. Its bark is beautifully striped in white and pale green and it usually makes a tree of
less than 20ft (6m) in height. It can be especially delightful in
winter when low-angle sunshine lights up the bark.

Very handsome in a different kind of way again is the weeping
willow-leaved pear, *Pyrus salicifolia* 'Pendula'. This grows some
15 to 20ft (4.5 to 6m) tall and forms a thick mat of pendulous
branches covered in silvery grey, willow-like leaves. This
distinctive tree will grow in any average, well-drained soil. I saw
recently a specimen of the oleaster, *Elaeagnus angustifolia,* growing near a *Pyrus salicifolia* 'Pendula' and it was suggested to me at
that time that, such is the resemblance, it would make an excellent
alternative to the latter, if such were needed. I'm inclined to
agree. The oleaster usually grows to around 20ft (6m) tall
–although it can be quite a lot more when especially well-suited
–and it has silvery-grey, willow-like leaves. It is of lax habit but not
fully weeping like the pyrus, however, and makes a somewhat
rounded head. It is more often grown as a large shrub, rather than
a small tree.

**The genus Sorbus**
The sorbuses – mostly belonging to the Aucuparia, or mountain
ash, section of the genus – include trees of special interest. *Sorbus*

Sorbus vilmorinii

*vilmorinii* perhaps more than most, for it is an elegant species (from western China) with typical, pretty, fern-like foliage which colours to shades of red and purple in autumn when the fruits are also an attraction, starting off red but fading with age to pink and rosy-white. It grows to a height of some 20ft (6m) and considerably less wide. The fruits are long-lasting so it offers especially good decorative value.

*Sorbus hupehensis* (from the same region as *S. vilmorinii*) is likely to be a little taller than the last and this has good decorative qualities in its purplish-brown stems, its leaves comprised of many leaflets of bluish-green colouring (which turn rich red in autumn) and white, long-lasting fruits which are suffused with pink. Although it can grow to 30ft (9m) or more tall the splendid variety 'Joseph Rock' has a pyramidal habit and is excellent for its autumn colour, the leaves turning to shades of orange and yellow and the fruits starting creamy-yellow and deepening to amber-yellow as they age. For a part of the garden where little lateral space is available there is also a fastigiate form of *S. aucuparia* available, *S. a.* 'Fastigiata', which makes a column up to 20 to 26ft (6 to 8m) tall. It carries bright red fruits.

All have white flowers which are borne in May or June, but it is the decorative features already stressed which earn them their place in gardens. All are easily pleased, growing well in any reasonable soil in sunshine or light shade.

**Bright foliage colour**
Two trees with golden foliage which cannot be left out of the reckoning even though they can, in favourable circumstances, make quite large trees are *Robinia pseudoacacia* 'Frisia' and *Gleditsia triacanthos* 'Sunburst' – the first being raised in Holland in the mid-1930s and the second in the United States in the mid-1950s. *R. pseudoacacia* 'Frisia' will in time make a tree of about 30ft (9m) in height and about half that in width; *G. triacanthos* 'Sunburst' rather more, and with, perhaps, this last having a rather better habit for the robinia is often a little untidy in its shape.

Still, 'Frisia' is a lovely tree and it is becoming more and more widely grown as gardeners appreciate that it holds its golden-yellow colouring right through from spring to autumn, when it assumes almost apricot tints before leaf fall. And yellow, as I suggested earlier in a brief comment on colour (see p. 22) is unrivalled for giving the garden a cheerful appearance. Like all the robinias, however, 'Frisia' has rather brittle branches, easily broken in windy conditions. It is happy in any ordinary, well-drained soil but it should be given a sunny, sheltered position for preference.

The same kind of conditions suit *G. triacanthos* 'Sunburst', the fern-like, pinnate leaves of which are a bright golden-yellow in spring, gradually assuming green tones as the season advances. To a certain extent the lateral spread of this tree can be controlled by judicious pruning, but if space is a cause of concern it is best to plump for 'Frisia' which is naturally narrower.

A splendid variegated holly for providing cheerful colour is *Ilex aquifolium* 'Golden Queen' which, despite its name, is a male form and therefore non-berrying. It more than makes up for this by the excellence of its foliage, for the bold, spiny leaves are dark green in colour with pale green and grey suffusions and a broad margin of rich yellow. It grows slowly to a height of around 18 to 20ft (5.5 to 6m), with a width of about half that, but to a degree its size can be contained by careful pruning in late summer. As a design feature the year round it is most valuable. The hollies generally are, of course, extremely easy-going plants growing well in any soil of reasonable quality. They will also succeed in sunshine or shade but it is best to give them good light if this is possible.

The sexes are divided in hollies, as I've already inferred, so to get female varieties to bear berries a male variety must be planted near by. If you have room for two specimens a good one to consider would be *I. altaclarensis* 'Golden King' which, believe it or not, is a female form (how 'Golden Queen' and 'Golden King' got such inappropriate names I have not been able to discover!). This is another very striking, golden-variegated holly, this time with virtually spineless leaves boldly margined with rich yellow. It bears large red berries, and its size roughly approximates to that of 'Golden Queen'. Do not overlook also the dwarf (2ft [60cm] tall and 3 to 4ft [1 to 1.75m] in width *I. crenata* 'Golden Gem' for this non-berrying form has golden-yellow colouring which develops best in a sunny position.

## Some more suggestions

The adaptability of the cotoneasters is especially marked; they will grow with gusto in any soil of average quality. It is best, however, to give them sunny positions whenever possible and that goes for the useful little *Cotoneaster* 'Hybridus Pendulus' which, when grown on a straight 6ft (2m) stem, makes a very attractive weeping specimen. It is the loveliest of sights in autumn when loaded with bright red berries. Such is the size of this weeping, evergreen tree that it can be fitted into virtually any garden – a height of about 10ft (3m) is its maximum, with a spread not exceeding this.

Willows need a soil which remains nicely moist and most of those making trees grow far too large for patio garden conditions. However, there is one which is suitable, the Kilmarnock willow, *Salix caprea* 'Kilmarnock' (formerly *S. caprea* 'Pendula') a form of our native goat willow which has an umbrella-like habit and does not usually exceed 10ft (3m) in height. It is now becoming more widely available. With its pendulous branches sweeping to the ground it makes a pleasing focal-point for a set-piece planting. Another very small weeping tree is the form of the copper beech

Above: Robinia
pseudoacacia *'Frisia', now a
very popular tree appreciated
for its leaf coloration.*

**Opposite:** *A delightful
association of laburnum and*
Clematis montana.

named *Fagus sylvatica* 'Purpurea Pendula', excellent for chalky soils, of course, and all others with the exception of those of a very heavy nature. In this case, too, the branches sweep to the ground and though it can make a tree 18ft (5.5m) tall it is often less. Its strong purple colouring makes it an excellent tree to associate with other plants which benefit from such contrasts. For instance, containers planted for spring display with daffodils or tulips and for summer display with rich red geraniums (pelargoniums, as they should really be called).

Seen at its best there is no more beautiful small tree than *Cercis siliquastrum*, the Judas tree (the common name alludes to the belief that it was from a specimen of this tree that Judas hanged himself). At most it makes a bushy-headed tree some 26ft (8m) tall, but it must have warmth, shelter and sunshine, combined with a good, well-drained soil, to flourish. A sandy loam is ideal. It is, therefore, a tree for the more climatically congenial parts of the country, and if it is grown in the North it needs the protection of a warm wall. Its glory is the mass of rosy-purple pea flowers which appear in May before the rounded, attractive leaves arrive. Later, the 4 to 5in (10 to 13cm) long, flat seed pods appear, these later taking on reddish-purple tints. The Judas tree is not among the easiest of trees to establish, and it should always be planted as a young specimen to give it the best chance of getting off to a good start.

I've left the laburnum until now, not because it is a tree I haven't much regard for (just the reverse) but because all parts are poisonous and particularly the seed pods, thus presenting a danger if there are young children in the family. If that is not a problem you need to take account of, then the laburnum is a tree which will grow well in any well-drained soil and in sunshine or light shade. The most spectacular is *Laburnum* x *watereri* 'Vossii' with especially long racemes of flowers which, in late May and early June, makes the common name for all laburnums of golden rain seem

particularly appropriate. It makes a tree eventually up to 35ft (10.6m) tall and perhaps 25ft (7.5m) wide. But do take heed of the problem I've mentioned. Numerous garden plants are poisonous but it is the attractiveness of the fallen seed pods to toddlers which is the problem.

## Conifers

Narrow-waisted conifers should not be overlooked either. In particular, ones like the ultra-narrow *Juniperus virginiana* 'Skyrocket' which grows up to 20ft (6m) and yet has a width of little over 1ft (30cm) can be very useful for providing added interest. The dark green Irish yew, *Taxus baccata* 'Fastigiata', as well, for this only grows about 15ft (4.5m) tall and 4ft (1.30m) wide and is available in a golden form, 'Fastigiata Aureomarginata', in which the leaves are margined with yellow. With both, the girth can increase quite a bit with age, but, like all yews they are slow growing. A small juniper which is proving very useful in patio gardens is *J. squamata* 'Blue Star'. It makes, eventually, a low bush about 3ft (1m) tall and 5ft (1.5m) wide of strong silvery-blue colouring. A very small and slow-growing Lawson cypress is *Chamaecyparis lawsoniana* 'Pygmaea Argentea', which makes a globe-shaped bush of great attraction, for the bluish-green foliage

**From left to right:**
Juniperus virginiana *'Skyrocket'*, Juniperus squamata *'Blue Star'*, Taxus baccata *'Fastigiata'*, Chamaecyparis lawsoniana *'Pygmaea Argentea'* and Chamaecyparis lawsoniana *'Ellwoodii'*.

is tipped with creamy-white. One or two specimens of these can be very effective in a patio setting. Both junipers and yews are happy on chalky soils.

Another Lawson cypress cultivar which you might well note for your patio garden is *Chamaecyparis lawsoniana* 'Ellwoodii', which grows slowly to a height of 8 to 10ft (2.5 to 3m) and has a width of about 3ft (1m). It is attractive, too, with its feathery, grey-green foliage, and puts on growth with the kind of slowness one finds so helpful with this type of gardening. This is even more true, too, of its form 'Ellwood's Gold', which grows to around 8ft (2.5m) tall and has yellow coloration, as the name suggests, to the extent that the growths are tipped with strong yellow, especially in summer. This is seen to best advantage if the plant gets plenty of exposure to sunshine. Generally speaking, though, the Lawson cypresses do equally well in sunshine or light shade, in any reasonably moist but well-drained, soil, but remember that any conifers of yellow colouring need plenty of sunshine to bring out that colour at its best.

It is in winter that one appreciates most of all the colouring and textures of conifers. I never tire of those in my own garden for their substance complements beautifully the airy tracery of the bare branches of deciduous trees in winter. In the context of the patio garden it will almost certainly be a case of at most two trees and perhaps one conifer, but what I have just said holds true.

# 5. Roses - the (Almost) Indispensable Ingredient

If there is one flower which is almost indispensable for patio garden display it must surely be the rose. Whether in the form of climbers for clothing walls and fences, pillars, poles or trellis work, bush (large-flowered or cluster-flowered bush roses as, officially, hybrid tea and floridunda roses are now to be called), shrub roses for beds, or miniatures for raised beds or containers, they are a delight for a good six months of the year.

Roses are the most long-suffering of plants, but this does not mean that they will not do far better if they are given that bit of extra attention, of thoughtful care. Prepare the ground well, and make sure that the drainage is as good as it can possibly be made. Both heavy and light soils can be improved by digging in peat or garden compost, if possible a couple of months in advance of planting. This last can be done at any time from late October until the end of March, although if you have the opportunity to plant at one end or the other of this season that is what I would advise. In any case, do not plant when the frost is in the soil or when it is wet and sticky. If your plants arrive from the nursery at such an inopportune time just store them in a cool but frost-proof place or heel them in out of doors, as I suggested for shrubs in similar circumstances (see p. 25). A few days before planting, too, I would advise forking into the planting beds a dressing of bonemeal at the rate of 4oz (110g) to the square yard. This slow-acting phosphatic fertilizer will be released to the plants over a long period.

You can, of course, plant container-grown roses at any time of year.

Roses – and especially those small-growing kinds mentioned above – look particularly effective when associated with paved

areas. The stark simplicity of the paving seems to throw into high relief the colour of the blooms; as it suits the stiff appearance of the roses' growth. It is best to grow large-flowered or cluster-flowered roses in open beds where they will get a free circulation of air around them and thus be less likely to succumb to that distressing and disfiguring ailment, mildew. This fungus disease thrives in airless conditions. You then leave the beds adjoining walls and fences for climbers of one kind or another.

### Climbers and ramblers

Ramblers have their place in the modern garden, things like the splendid old 'Albéric Barbier' (good for a north or east wall), whose creamy-white flowers have been enjoyed in gardens since the start of the century and 'Sanders' White' which have been around for almost as long, but it is the climbing roses of the present day like 'Pink Perpêtue', the cream, flushed rosy-pink 'Handel' (especially fine, see illustration) and the orange-scarlet 'Danse du Feu' which, with others like them, are so admirably suited for clothing pillars and poles with glorious colour to a height, on average, of 7 to 8ft (2.3 to 2.5m). Others which I would especially commend are the pink, salmon-shaded, double 'Aloha', especially to be commended for its fragrance and ability to withstand wet weather as well as its attractive foliage; the pink, semi-double, 'Bantry Bay'; the crimson 'Hamburger Phoenix', also semi-double; and the flesh pink 'New Dawn', this last an old-stager which is one parent of 'Pink Perpêtue', the other being 'Danse du Feu'. The varieties 'Hamburger Phoenix' and 'Danse du Feu' will do well against north or east walls.

For warm walls I can thoroughly recommend a very lovely old China rose, 'Mutabilis' ('Tipo Ideale') which makes a superb specimen so grown, coming into flower in June and producing the most lovely crop of single flowers which are coppery-red in the bud, open to yellow, then turn pink and red. The effect, overall, is very beautiful. After the main flowering, more blooms are produced in lesser numbers. A warm wall is, however, essential for it to do well.

*Rose 'Handel'*

When it won the Royal National Rose Society's Henry Edland Memorial Medal for the most fragrant new rose of its year (in 1973) the variety 'Compassion' was the first climbing rose ever to win that coveted award – and it is, at the time of writing, a record which still stands. Its double blooms are pale salmon-pink in colour with rich organge shading, and it grows to a height of 8 to 10ft (2.5 to 3m). It is a rose to keep in mind when you are next thinking of making additions to the garden. So is its primrose-yellow sport 'Highfield'.

The exquisite, miniature-flowered 'Climbing Cécile Brunner' has small pink blooms which are a lovely sight when matched with a warm-pink brick wall. This old rose, also repeat flowering, has been grown in gardens since 1894 and long may it continue to be so. It is very beautiful, and grows up to 20ft tall (6m). Another fine old climber, 'Phyllis Bide', which will reach to a height of 10ft (3m) or more, produces its pale yellow, pink-flushed blooms over most of summer. I cannot understand why it is so little grown for it is extremely attractive.

Another repeat flowerer is the *bracteata* climber 'Mermaid', but do no attempt to grow this rose unless you can provide a warm,

*Rose 'Mermaid'*

*Rose 'Silver Jubilee'*

**Opposite:** *'Matangi', a striking cluster-flowered rose.*

sheltered wall facing south. The delectable, single, primrose-yellow blooms with prominent amber-yellow stamens are fully 4in (10cm) across.

The cautionary note I have struck is necessary, for this is a rose which can be damaged by severe frost. Its vigour is not in doubt, however, for here we have a rose which will grow to 26 to 30ft (8 to 9m) tall and demands a house wall to do it justice. Then you can expect to enjoy the flowers for a couple of months in mid-summer and again in autumn – but it is not, I repeat, a rose for less favoured parts of the country.

**Bush roses**

Almost tailor-made for patio gardens, of course, are low-growing cluster-flowered cultivars – roses like the orange-red 'Topsi' (which won the R.N.R.S. President's International Trophy – the top award – in 1972); salmon-pink 'Tip Top'; pale pink 'Gentle Touch' and yellow 'Bright Smile'; orange, golden-tinted 'Sweet Magic'; scarlet 'Wee Jock', 'Marlena', and 'Trumpeter'; 'Regensberg', pink and white, and the apricot 'Peek A Boo'. Add to these the orange-red 'Anna Ford' and you have a good idea of the choice available. Their modest height makes them especially good for patio display, and, like all cluster-flowered roses, they are free-flowering.

Other fine cluster-flowered roses for the patio are the attractive 'Anisley Dickson', pink, with reddish-salmon overtones, and winner in 1984 of the R.N.R.S. President's International Trophy; 'Korresia' with shapely, fragrant, bright yellow flowers; 'Fragrant Delight', salmon-pink and well-scented as the name implies; and that fine white 'Iceberg', introduced in 1958 and still among the best – white is always a good colour to introduce into the garden, both for its own sake and as a foil for other colours – the salmon 'City of Leeds'; golden-yellow 'Allgold' and crimson-red 'The Times'.

Others of special interest are the tallish, apricot-orange 'Southampton', with good fragrance; 'Eye Paint', with single scarlet blooms with a white eye and boss of yellow staments; 'Matangi', orange-vermilion, shaded silver at the base of the petals; and 'Margaret Merril', pale pink overlying white and sweetly scented.

It would be impossible to leave the cluster-flowered roses without saying something about two splendid cultivars, one of which was introduced in 1982 and the other a real veteran. They are 'Mountbatten', a tall cultivar with shapely buds which open to double flowers of a fetching primrose-yellow. It grows up to 5ft (1.5m) tall. The other rose is the very familiar 'Queen Elizabeth' which can top 6ft (2m) in some situations. It is still a fine and very popular rose with its lovely clear pink flowers and good foliage. One or two specimens of either of these cultivars would make a delightful feature if you sited them

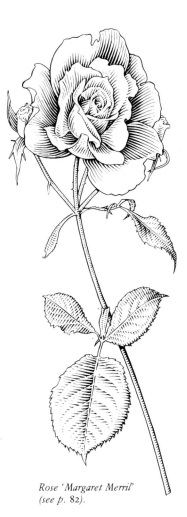

*Rose 'Margaret Merril'*
*(see p. 82).*

with care. 'Mountbatten' was voted 'Rose of the Year' in 1982 by British rose growers and breeders.

Two old polyantha roses which have much to offer are 'Nathalie Nypels' and 'The Fairy'. The first is a rose with much charm, its rose-pink, double flowers being borne on a spreading bush some 2ft (60cm) tall. 'The Fairy' has unfailing attraction for most of us with its small, double flowers being borne in great abundance from mid-summer onwards. It also is spreading and with a height of 2½ft (75cm).

The large-flowered bush rose 'Silver Jubilee', of compact habit, was the 1977 winner of the R.N.R.S. President's International Trophy already referred to in other connections. The flowers are a lovely combination of pink, apricot, peach and cream. It is also a very disease-resistant rose.

Other large-flowered bush roses of special worth are 'Alec's Red', with flowers of rich cherry-red and with what I would call a "tidy" habit; 'Alexander', orange-vermilion; 'Grandpa Dickson', a good yellow which fades to a paler colour and becomes pink at the edges of the petals; 'Piccadilly', scarlet and yellow; the coral-salmon 'Mischief'; dusky red 'Fragrant Cloud', salmon-pink 'Paul Shirville', and the legendary 'Peace', if you can accommodate its large frame and so enjoy its pale yellow blooms, edge with pink.

Some of the cluster-flowered and large-flowered bush roses I have just mentioned are available as standard specimens, and these can be used to good effect in the patio garden. A certain number of roses are available, too, as weeping standards, which can be extremely attractive. These include the ramblers 'Crimson Shower'; rose-pink 'Dorothy Perkins'; creamy-white 'Albéric Barbier'; and coppery-pink 'Albertine'.

## Shrub roses

The modern shrub roses, like the tallest of the bush roses, can be used only with discretion in the patio garden, perhaps in ones or twos; but do consider making a set-piece planting of the creamy-white, 4ft (1.25m) tall 'Sally Holmes', or the vermilion-orange 'Fred Loads', which smothers its 6ft (2m) frame with its single blooms. And if you want a good yellow you can always turn to that excellent cultivar 'Chinatown'.

Quite my favourite shrub rose for planting near paving is the striking 'Ballerina" a spreading bush some 3 to 4ft (1 to 1.3m) tall. It is of hydrid musk ancestry with attractive pale green foliage and carries in summer masses of pale pink, white-eyed flowers in bold clusters. The effect is striking and especially so when it sweeps its growths out over paving. 'Marjorie Fair', bred from 'Ballerina', is its deep red equivalent and a very lovely rose indeed. Other shrub roses of special worth are the rich yellow, full-petalled 'Graham Thomas'; long-flowering 'Golden Wings', with single pale yellow flowers, set off by amber stamens; and 'Robusta', scarlet. These last two are especially long floweirng. All of them grow about 4ft (1.3m) tall.

Whatever roses you choose to grow, though — and that is very much a matter of personal preference – pay particular attention to the colour blending. Some modern roses have quite strong colours and carelessness can lead to some unfortunate juxtapositions.

## Miniature roses

I've left until last a group of roses which are rapidly increasing in popularity, the miniatures; none of them are over 1½ft (45cm) tall and most are under 15in (38cm) with blooms in proportion to their overall size. For raised patio beds they are ideal. The wide range of cultivars includes 'Royal Salute', a rose-pink variety which I am growing in just the kind of conditions suggested; the salmon-flowered 'Angela Rippon', 'Starina', orange-scarlet; 'Pour Toi', cream; 'Sweet Fairy', lilac-pink; 'Coralin', orange-red; and 'Perla de Alcanada', crimson. There are numerous others. What they must be given is a position where their size will seem in scale with their surroundings. Apart from narrow raised beds, they are, of course, admirable for growing in containers. But if you grow them in tubs, sinks or other containers, make sure that they have a good depth of compost to grow in and that they do not lack food or moisture. Make sure also that the soil drainage is adequate. When they are grown in pots (which is also a possibility) do not treat them as house plants apart from, perhaps, taking them indoors for the brief spell when they are at the height of their flowering. Plunge the pots to their rims in soil in the garden after they have done their stint in this way.

## A guide to pruning

Pruning is a chore which always confuses the newcomer to gardening, and that is not surprising. But really it is a very straightforward job once the underlying principles are understood.

Let us take the large-flowered bush roses first. With these one is pruning for shapeliness, good health and quality – rather than quantity – of bloom. The degree of pruning given – heavy, medium or light – depends on the vigour of the variety, and that also goes for the cluster-flowered bush roses, which I shall come to in a moment. Plants which are hard pruned will make more growth than those lightly pruned, so it follows that strong-growing varieties need lighter pruning than others. In practice it will be found that most roses need only moderate pruning. Don't go mad with the secateurs.

Newly planted roses need quite different treatment in this respect to established specimens. In the March following the

*Rose 'Albéric Barbier'*
*(see p. 80).*

85

*Opposite: The cluster-flowered rose 'Mountbatten' – worthy holder of a great name.*

**Left:** *'The Fairy', almost indispensable for providing colour from mid-summer onwards.*

planting of large-flowered bush roses, or immediately of course if you plant at the end of the planting season, cut back the shoots to within two or three 'eyes' (the gardening term for dormant buds) of the base.

Thereafter, prune in March (although see what I have to say on p. 89 about the different views on when to prune) so that the growth made in the previous year is reduced by about half, while taking account of what I said earlier about adjusting the degree of pruning to the needs of the particular variety. The aim is to produce an open-centred bush to which light and air will have free access, which is healthy – all dead or weak wood should be

*Miniature rose 'Pour Toi' (see p. 85).*

cut away at this time — and which will bear flowers of high quality. When pruning, always cut to an outward pointing bud or eye, and make the cut cleanly, say about ¼ in (0.6cm) above — in other words, leave no snags to later die back and cause further trouble. Make the cut in such a way that it slopes from just above the bud to lower down on the opposite side of the shoot. The importance of having really sharp secateurs should not need emphasising.

With newly planted cluster-flowered bush roses where the objectives are rather different — with these roses you get more colour over a longer period but not the perfection of bloom of the hybrid teas — cut back the shoots to within four or five eyes of the base, again in the March following planting.

Allowing that there are large-, medium- and small-growing cluster-flowered, bush roses, one prunes to produce a freer-growing bush than with the large-flowered type, so pruning is lighter. After the initial treatment just outlined, the annual treatment in March could consist of cutting out some of the oldest wood to within two or three eyes of the base, and then cutting back one-year-old laterals by rather more or less than half, depending on the vigour of the variety. New growths which arise from the base should be pruned very lightly indeed.

Treat standard specimens of both types in exactly the same way as their bush counterparts so far as pruning is concerned, and weeping standards like the ramblers or repeat-flowering climbers of which these are special forms, budded on to 5 or 6ft (1.5 or 2m) stems.

Newly-planted climbing and rambler roses should have their growths left at full length. Established specimens of these roses — which need quite different treatment — should be dealt with in the following manner.

Thereafter, with *wichuraiana* ramblers, which throw up new canes from the base each summer to bear the next year's crop of flowers, cut out the flowered growths to the base as soon as flowering has finished, and tie the new shoots in their place. With other ramblers, which do not make new shoots from the base annually and often develop growth higher up the sterms, confine your attentions to removing any dead shoots and unwanted wood and occasionally cutting straggly shoots back to a dormant bud low down on the stems, again when flowering has finished.

Modern repeat-flowering climbers should have their shoots just lightly tipped after planting and thereafter, in subsequent years — like the ramblers just referred to — be given practically no pruning, except for any necessary cutting back of old wood and, of course, the removal of dead and diseased wood.

Climbing sorts of large-flowered and cluster-flowered bush roses need treating with special care for they are very prone to reversion to bush form if pruning is mishandled. Again, with these, just lightly tip the shoots after planting — in March — and in subsequent years confine any pruning to the removal of dead or weak wood and the cutting of the lateral growth on mature shoots to about four buds from the main stem.

Modern shrub roses, like the shrub roses of older vintage — the old-fashioned roses as they are called — need very little pruning, either after planting or in the years to come. Just prune to remove dead or weak wood and to keep them within bounds. The same applies also to the delightful little miniature roses.

I said earlier that there are different views about when it is best to prune. Some gardeners, especially those living in climatically favoured areas, prefer mid-winter pruning which provides earlier growth and earlier flowers. They are taking a gamble with the weather, which for them may be fully justified. I think that for most of us it is best to wait until the time I have suggested, March, or possibly February, which again could be just the right time in some districts. It is all a matter of opinion, like so much else in gardening. The trouble is that our climate is fickle and early-stimulated growth can be damaged by a side-swipe from the weather.

Pruning is one aspect of making sure that you get the kind of performance from your roses you always hope to enjoy. There are others, like mulching and feeding, dead-heading, the removal of suckers and pest and disease control.

## General care

With pruning out of the way and the prunings consigned to the bonfire, it will soon be time to think of applying a mulch, especially important on lightish soils which dry out quickly in warm, sunny weather. It is best to wait until the soil has had a chance to warm up though before applying such material around the plants. You can use peat, composted bark, garden compost or, if you can lay your hands on it, well rotted farmyard manure, preferably horse manure, which would, of course, provide the plants with food as well as slowing down moisture losses from the soil. To give you some idea of the kind of quantity of manure you would need, one barrowload of manure is enough to cover 10 to 12 square yards (8.36 to 10.03m²) of ground.

If you are using peat, composted bark or garden compost — you may be able to suitably camouflage a compost bin in a corner of the patio, and with effecent compost accelerators waste vegetation can soon be turned into useful material — add first a dressing of a proprietary rose fertiliser, as directed by the makers, so that the plants will get supplies of a balanced feed during the period of the year when they most need such help. Make the mulch several inches thick.

A mulch then is extremely effective in cutting down moisture losses from the soil, but do not be misled into thinking that it

absolves you from watering at all. In warm, dry spells, and indeed at intervals anyway, draw back some of the mulching material and make sure that the soil is not dry underneath. If is is, then soak the ground thoroughly for to do less is useless.

Dead-heading, a curious term which is in fact very descriptive, is the gardener's way of talking about the removal of dead flowers. With roses, this is something one should do frequently, especially in the patio garden, not only because it will encourage further flowering but also because the sight of dead rose blooms hanging forlornly on the bushes is hardly inspiring. Cut to an

*'Majorie Fair', a very lovely
shrub rose of rich colouring.*

outward pointing bud, as I have recommended for pruning, for
in its way this is what dead-heading is, and remove as short a
piece of stem as possible each time.

Suckers can be an infernal nuisance, as we all know, particularly with bush roses and standards, and if you are not sure if a
shoot is a sucker or not, follow it down to its point of origin.
Suckers originate from the rootstock on which the particular
cultivar has been budded, and where they are identified as such,
either by the means I have just outlined or by their distinctive
appearance — different leaf colour, shape and size, and the prickly

nature of the stems — pull them out without delay. And pull is the operative word (if this is possible), for if one resorts to cutting them off there is a strong possibility that more will come in their place.

**Pests and disease**

I don't want to dwell too long on pests and diseases, but obviously these must be given consideration if you are going to enjoy healthy plants.

Of the pests, watch out particularly for greenfly infestations. These you can combat with an insecticide like pirimicarb, derris or malathion. Caterpillars of various kinds, for which permethrin is an effective deterrent, should also be watched for, and small numbers can of course, be dispatched in the time-honoured way — by hand picking. You can spray against leaf hoppers with permethrin or pirimiphos-methyl, and the latter insecticides will also control the leaf-rolling sawfly, if you apply it early enough in the season, before the leaves have become tightly curled to provide a protective armour and food for the developing larvae.

Gamma HCH and dimethoate are effective against those other pests, the easily recognisable cuckoo spit — the insect, the frog-hopper, makes frothy, spittle-like mounds on the plants — and thrips or thunderflies, as they are called, which make a special point of damaging the blooms, especially in the bud stage. In the latter case alternatives are malathion or pirimiphos-methyl.

Mildew, the fungus disease which is a universal problem and to which some varieties of rose are particularly prone, is, alas, only too easily identified with the white or greyish mould coating the leaves and stems as well as the flower buds. Wide fluctuations in temperature, poor soil drainage and dryness at the roots, over-lush growth brought about by incorrect feeding, and damp, stagnant air are all conditions which encourage this disease to take a hold. It is best to get your blow in first and make pre-emptive sprayings at intervals in summer with bupirimate plus triforine, propiconazole or benomyl, applied strictly in accordance with the manufacturer's instructions, as all such garden chemicals must be.

And now for that other major trouble of roses, black spot. This is one case where the gardener is a clean-air district comes off worse than the townsman who suffers the disadvantage of rather polluted air. This disease does not find sulphur-laden air at all to its liking.

Black spot is immediately recognizable by the black markings which form on the leaves. These spots spread with great rapidity and often cause premature defoliation wtih all that that means for the health of the plant. Fallen leaves affected by black spot should always be collected and burnt, for the spores remain active and can come through the winter to start the whole sorry cycle off again in spring, when the new leaves form. The answer, if you live in an area likely to be troubled by this disease, is again to take pre-emptive action by spraying with bupirimate plus triforine, propiconazole, benomyl or other recommended chemicals as directed by the manufacturers. In winter you can also spray with Bordeaux mixture to kill the over-wintering spores on the plant and in the soil.

Black spot, mildew, rust and aphids can be dealt with at the same time by applying, once every 10 to 14 days from April, the systemic fungicide/aphicide Roseclear. This contains the insecticide pirimicarb and the fungicides bupirimate and triforine. A real advantage is that the aphicide, while killing aphids quickly, leaves beneficial insects like ladybirds unharmed.

Take preventive action also against that other serious rose trouble, rose rust, which is seen as rust-coloured pustules on the undersides of the leaves from early in the season. Remove and burn all affected parts of the plant as soon as seen. The fungicides mancozeb and bupirimate plus triforine can also be used, as directed by the manufacturer.

When canker occurs – it often follows bad pruning, gaining entry through snags, etc. – cut away the diseased wood immediately and destroy it by buring. There is no chemical control. If the pruning cuts are more than ½ m (1cm) in diameter than a wound dressing should be applied as a preventative measure.

Of course there are other rose troubles of a less important nature, but the last thing I want to do is to give the impression that roses are accident-prone semi-invalids. You will know that they are not, in any case, but by the same token it is only common sense to keep a wary eye open for the troubles I have enumerated.

# 6. Making Good Use of Perennials

Stachys
macrantha
superba

**Opposite:** *Nothing could emphasise more dramatically than this tub-grown* Hosta *'Thomas Hogg' the fine decorative qualities of so many members of this genus.*

I have been more than pleased to note in recent years a strong resurgence of interest in herbaceous perennial plants, and not so much for massed effect (although that can be stunning if you have room for an extensive border or island beds, as you certainly haven't in the patio garden) as for providing small pockets of interest and colour in all manner of different settings. The free-style use of this fascinating group of plants has given them a completely new lease of life.

It may be a small thing, too, but there is a great deal of pleasure to be gained from following their progress from the first tentative signs of growth in spring to flowering and their dying down in autumn. Some, like the hostas, paeonies and montbretias, take on lovely leaf colours in autumn – yellows, ochres, and russety-browns – which add a great deal to the enjoyment of the garden at that time. You can experience all this too on the small intimate scale of your patio garden.

## The importance of foliage

If you have never given the matter a thought it might seem an extraordinary thing to say, but leaf textures and shapes and, of course, their colours, can give as much pleasure as flowers in a different way. Flowers are essential, but they are only one part of the equation in creating an integrated, satisfying garden.

A perennial I especially value (and excellent for the kind of use we are considering) is a plant called *Stachys macrantha superba* which creates a low carpet of dark green with its broadly ovate leaves, wrinkled all over their surface like the weather-beaten face of an old countryman – a delightful base from which to throw up the whorls of rosy-mauve flowers in early summer. For half the year it provides excellent ground cover. The hostas have the most alluring leaf shapes and colours, and, in a completely different way, who could not appreciate the winsome charm of the

94

little epimediums with their heart-shaped leaves suspended on wire-like stems – the picture of elegance. Then there is that iris which the flower arrangers love to raid for stems – *Iris pallida variegata*, the sword-like, 2 to 3ft (60cm to 1m) leaves of which have a ground colour of soft grey and, depending on whether it is the yellow or the white form, bold longitudinal stripes of one or other of those colours. These forms are often identified in plant catalogues and elsewhere as *aureo-variegata* and *argenteo-variegata*, if not just as *variegata* with a colour description.

And so one could go on, but I think I've said enough to make the point. Do give foilage the attention it deserves. Before turning to the plants and what they can do for us in intimate patio conditions let us consider the basis of their cultivation.

### Care of perennials

Most perennials need lifting and dividing about once every third or fourth year, in spring or autumn, for the clumps become overcrowded and too spreading and will almost certainly have lost vigour and quality to an unacceptable extent. It is an easy enough job to do and I will come to that in a moment, but the point I want to make now is that, once these plants are in the ground there is really nothing you can do in the way of real soil improvement for that very considerable length of time. So, get the drainage of the soil, its texture and so on right before you start. Both soils which are too light and so lack body and moisture-retentive qualities, and soil which is too heavy and perhaps is too slow to rid itself of excess moisture can be improved by digging in peat, composted bark or garden compost. Take care also to clear the ground of all perennial weeds before planting, as far as this is possible.

Still, with regard to this periodical lifting and dividing which is so beneficial for most plants, remember that there are those, like the paeonies, Japanese anemones, hellebores and oriental poppies, which do not take kindly to disturbance. They will take time to settle down and you may not get them to flower again for a couple of years, perhaps even longer.

The lifted clumps can be levered apart by placing two forks back to back through the lifted clump and forcing the handles outwards, if you cannot achieve the same end with your hands or a hand fork, as you can with smaller plants. It is the younger, outer part of the plant which is the most useful for re-planting, for the heart of the clump will often be exhausted.

Other cultural points with perennials: if they need to be staked, do this early, before wind and rain have caused any damage, and if they are of the kind which make new growths very prolifically, reduce these in number early in the season also so that better quality blooms will be obtained by concentrating the energies of the plant.

96

### Perennials in mixed planting schemes

Another thing you can do with much success is to mix perennials with selected annuals, biennials and bulbous flowers as well as with the odd shrub or two to get the best of all possible worlds. Let us consider those perennials that I believe are of special relevance to this type of garden.

I have already mentioned hostas in passing – the plaintain lilies as they are often called – and these with their bold foliage and spikes of lily-like trumpet flowers in summer in colours from mauve to lilac and white have much to offer. They associate so well with paving and, being clump forming, make features in their own right for a good six months of the year.

Those I particularly like in *Hosta crispula*, *H. undulata* and *H. fortunei albopicta*, and I will briefly outline the attractions of each. *Hosta crispula* is perhaps my favourite, a species up to a foot (30cm) tall with handsome tapered leaves of rich green with broad white margins of indeterminate width. Its lavender-coloured flowers, on 2½ft (75cm) stems, arrive about mid-summer and last for several weeks. *H. undulata*, as its name implies, has leaves with wavy surfaces, in this case of clear green marked with a central band of creamy-white, and lilac flowers which it bears on 2 to 2½ft (60 to 75cm) stems. This makes a mat of foliage less than 1ft (30cm) tall. The third of my trio, *H. fortunei albopicta*, has broad leaves which begin life bright yellow edged with pale green and age to predominantly pale green with a darker green edging. It is very impressive and some 2ft (60cm) tall. This too has lilac flowers in mid-summer.

Hostas like light shade and a moisture-retaining soil of, for preference, a loamy texture. If the soil is lacking in substance then dig in plenty of peat before planting, something which can be done at any time from October to March, when the weather is suitable. I consider these among the best of all ground-cover plants and there are many to choose from.

Another very useful and exceedingly pretty perennial which is completely at home in association with paving is the lady's mantle, *Alchemilla mollis*, a plant with light green, rounded leaves with scalloped edges above which ride billowing sprays of delicate-looking little greenish-yellow star flowers in June and July. No wonder it is so loved by the flower arrangers – it is the epitome of grace. Only 1 to 1½ft (30 to 45cm) tall, it forms solid ground-covering clumps in sunshine or light shade and it will grow happily in most well-drained soils, preferably rather moist (which need not be a contradiction in terms).

For space-effectiveness also I would give top marks to the herbaceous geraniums or crane's bills – the true geraniums, not the pot-grown and bedding pelargoniums which, confusingly, have geranium as their common name – for these provide splendid ground cover, are adaptable, have delightful flowers,

Alchemilla mollis, *associated here, most effectively, with the small-growing cluster-flowered rose 'Golden Slippers'.*

which in some kinds are very long lasting and often very attractive foliage. Paragons of virtue, in other words.

A particularly attractive one is *Geranium psilostemon* which, in early summer, is a picture with its bushy, 2½ft (75cm) frame a mass of deeply cut leaves, above which are carried a mantle of the most lovely magenta-red, black-centred flowers. Another I consider outstanding is *G. endressii* 'A. T. Johnson' for, on clumps only 1½ft (45cm) tall, this bears masses of silvery-pink blooms over a long period in summer. Others of special note include 'Johnson's Blue', early summer flowering and with deeply cut foliage, and atractive *G. sanguineum lancastriense splendens*, a variety of the bloody crane's bill which grows some 10in (25cm)

Geranium sanguineum
lancastriense splendens

tall and flowers practically the summer through, its pretty
blooms being pale pink in colour with red veining. Shorter still
at 4in (10cm) is the very pretty 'Ballerina' which bears red-
veined, lilac-pink flowers in the first half of summer.

You can grow most herbaceous geraniums in any well-drained
soil in sun or shade, although the last-mentioned cultivar does
best in sun. There are many more from which to make a choice.

Fine perennials, too, for the patio bed are the mat-forming
*Polygonum affine* 'Donald Lowndes' and the better known *P. a.*
'Darjeeling Red'. Of the two the best is undoubtedly the more
compact 'Donald Lowndes' which bears its pretty deep pink
flower spikes on 8 to 10in (20 to 25cm) stems over a long period in

*Polygonum affine 'Donald Lowndes' (see p. 99).*

summer above attractive fresh green, narrow leaves which form a solid mat of growth. By autumn the flowers have deepened in colour to a russety red. 'Darjeeling Red', a little taller, starts to bear its deep rose-pink flowers a little later in the season. Both retain their leaves into winter, when they turn a pleasant warm brown colour. A moist soil is a "must", combined with good drainage. With this can go a position in sun or light shade.

For a delightful early summer show there are few plants to beat the oriental poppies (varieties of *Papaver orientale*), if they are given a sunny site and an average soil with good drainage. They come into flower in late May and continue through June, and although they take up quite a bit of room and are not an asset out of flower I would still find room myself for at least a couple of plants of, say, the orange-scarlet, black-blotched 'Marcus Perry', 'Perry's White' or the rich scarlet 'Goliath'. These are all 2½ to 3ft (75cm to 1m) tall.

A dicentra which adds distinction to any border in early summer is *Dicentra spectabilis*, the bleeding heart or Dutchman's breeches, for it bears the most lovely locket-like rose-red flowers which hang in arched stems above deeply cut foliage. It is some 2ft (60cm) tall.

A hybrid dicentra which I am sure is going to have a bright future is 'Pearl Drops', only 10in (25cm) tall and with a mass of bluish-yellow divided leaves above which are borne, from May until early autumn, a mass of white flowers. It is a real asset where space demands that every plant must earn its keep.

Another excellent perennial which makes a feature in its own right or a delightful companion for numerous other flowers is *Salvia superba*. This makes a bold clump of growth some 3ft (1m) tall and is a splendid sight in the second half of summer when bearing its spikes of purple flowers above sage-like leaves. It is a perfect companion, for instance, for the similarly sized *Achillea* 'Coronation Gold' which bears large, flat-topped golden yellow flowers at the same time. Both need lots of sunshine and a well-drained soil.

Other strong candidates for space in the patio garden are the Japanese anemones (forms of *Anemone hybrida*) providing colour from the beginning of August until the end of September. With a height of 2½ to 3ft (75cm to 1m) there are many situations where these look just right, and good varieties include the white 'Louise Uhink', pink 'Queen Charlotte' and the similarly coloured 'September Charm'. They like moist soil conditions and light shade, but are very easy going.

Perhaps one of the best of all herbaceous plants, though (certainly among the smaller ones), is *Coreopsis verticillata* for it literally smothers its bushy mound of leaves, only 1½ft (45cm) tall, with bright yellow daisy flowers from early to late summer. It's a plant for a sunny position and preferably a light soil.

What else? The bergenias — which used to be called megaseas and before that saxifrages, as they still are by some people – gardeners either love or hate. Maybe they have got leathery, rather cabbage-like leaves, as the unkind say, but what superb ground-cover plants they are, and how handsome are their bold flower trusses composed of many bell-shaped flowers. As the foliage is evergreen too, you have cover throughout the year, and the leaves of some like 'Ballawley' turn to reddish shades in winter.

'Ballawley' is in fact a particularly fine hybrid with very large leaves and rose-red flowers in April and May. The popular *B. cordifolia* has heart-shaped leaves and bears rose-coloured blooms in March and April, while the white-flowered 'Silberlicht' is another whose foliage may take on reddish tones in winter. All these grow about 1ft (30cm) tall. They will grow in almost any soil, in sun or shade.

For placing on their own, say around the base of a small tree which does not cast too much shade, and the soil is of a lightish nature, you could make a nice show with *Heuchera* 'Bressingham Hybrids'. Above a thick cover of rounded leaves in summer floats a hazy mass of tiny flowers, borne in panicles on 2½ to 3ft (75cm to 1m) stems in colours from pink to rich red. As the foliage

Salvia superba *(left) and* Achillea *'Coronation Gold'*

of these too is evergreen, they give good year-round ground cover. So do the little epimediums with their wiry-stemmed, heart-shaped leaves, and in spring appear delicate spikes of wispy flowers in yellow, pink or red. These love light shade and a reasonably good soil, and the ones to go for, at any rate in my opinion, are the yellow-flowered *Epimedium perralderianum*, the coppery-red *E. warleyense* and *E. macranthum* 'Rose Queen', another good red.

Tall bearded irises have a short flowering season, but how beautiful they are in late May and June. Their bold sword-like foliage can also, I believe, be turned to good use at other times if they are associated with the right plants to form a contrast. The important thing with these is to give them a position where the soil is fairly light and well drained, and to take care when planting not to set the rhizomes too deeply in the ground. Their tops should be just level with the surface of the soil and you orientate them facing south so that they get the maximum amount of sunshine which is available. You can plant them in June (immediately after flowering), in September or in March.

I mentioned earlier *Iris pallida variegata* (see p. 96) but that is a plant you grow more for its striking foliage effect than the display put on in mid-summer by its blue flowers. With the lovely winter-flowering Algerian iris, *I. unguicularis* (which many, understandably, still persist in calling by its much prettier old name of *I. stylosa*), it's a different matter, for the flowers of this 2ft (60cm) tall plant are very beautiful indeed and are borne intermittently during mild weather right through from autumn to spring.

*Iris unguicularis* needs a lean soil with really sharp drainage, and a sunny, sheltered position, too, not because it isn't hardy (even though it occurs in nature in Algeria and a wide spread of the eastern Mediterranean) but because the flowers can be so easily damaged by frost and rough weather. These flowers are somewhat variable in colour for there are numerous forms in commerce (few of them named) ranging from very pale lavender-blue to much deeper shades. All are delightful, although I like the deeper coloured ones best myself, and the blooms of all are a joy for cutting for room decoration. It is a plant to site against a house wall, preferably near a door you use frequently so that you enjoy its beauty to the full. I have mentioned that it should be given a lean soil. If it is richly fed it will, like annual flowers, tend to concentrate on producing foliage at the expense of flowers.

Since so many good colours have become available in the hemerocallises or day-lilies (their flowers, individually, last for only one day, although produced in succession over a long period, from June to August) they have become increasingly popular. They are so accommodating, growing well in any

Opposite: Sedum *'Autumn Joy'*, a delight in early autumn.

Bergenia *'Ballawley'* (see p. 101).

Iris unguicularis
*(see p. 103).*

ordinary, well-drained soil in sunshine or light shade, but nevertheless appreciating soil with plenty of goodness in it.

Quite apart from the lily-like flowers in their yellows, creams, diverse reds, pinks, oranges and so on, the bold clumps of arched, rush-like foliage which they throw up can be used to great effect as a contrast to the colourings and forms of other near-by plants. In spring, the young foliage is a very pale green colour, which can be strikingly effective. Of the many cultivars offered, nearly all in the 2 to 3ft (60cm to 1m) height range, three of special note are the deep red 'Stafford', 'Pink Damask' and 'Hyperion', clear yellow. The recently introduced 1¾ft (55cm) tall 'Stella D'Oro' with canary-yellow flowers is ideal for patio planting.

Herbaceous paeonies take up quite a lot of room, but again I consider their foliage very decorative and if you plant something like the 3ft (1m) tall 'Bowl of Beauty' you can enjoy those large, rosy-pink, cream-centred blooms in June and July and then appreciate afterwards the matronly spread of greenery. As I said earlier, too, the leaves colour up nicely in the autumn. They like good soil and sunshine.

For edging paths remember, too, the catmint, *Nepeta faassenii* – better known, if incorrectly, as *N. mussinii* – which is only a foot (30cm) tall and so useful in producing its lavender-mauve flowers above grey-green foliage the summer through in any ordinary soil, in sun or shade. It also associates very well with roses. For a sunny, sheltered position, too, why not find a home for that lovely, very architectural spurge *Euphorbia characias* whose great heads of greenish-yellow flowers in early summer look so imposing above the ranks of bluish-grey leaves. This spurge is worth a prominent position on its own, preferably in a spot where you can see it from a window of the house. The similar-looking sub-shrubby *E. wulfenii* is another to consider, and this stays in flower for a longer period. Any well-drained soil of reasonable quality will suit these two.

If in shrubs one tends to look on the excellent *Senecio* 'Sunshine' (see p. 44) as the most useful of all grey-foliaged subjects, so in herbaceous perennials I would let my thoughts turn to that excellent variety of the wormwood *Artemisia absinthium*, named 'Lambrook Silver', which was introduced by that great gardener, the late Mrs Margery Fish, who created at East Lambrook Manor, her Somerset home, such a Mecca for gardeners. The filigree of silver foliage put up by this 3ft (1m) tall plant is a constant delight, and a marvellous foil for many other plants which share its liking for a sunny position and really good soil drainage. It looks delightful, for instance, in association with the very beautiful *Aster frikartii* which produces its lavender-blue ray-flowers with gold yellow centres from July into autumn. It is of similar height to 'Lambrook Silver'.

This aster also looks stunning with *Rudbeckia fulgida* 'Goldsturm', the 2ft (60cm) variety of Black-eyed Susan, which smothers itself with its golden-yellow, black-centred ray-flowers from July to September. It is, of course, another sun-lover.

Another plant for a sunny, well-drained position which can be rewarding in patio conditions is the 2ft (60cm) tall gayfeather, *Liatris spicata*, which opens up its tufty mauvish-pink flower spikes from the top downwards. It, too, flowers from July to September and it is best in its variety 'Kobold', in which the colour is more intense – a nice plant to have near-by when you are sitting out at that time of year.

Several stonecrops or sedums are really lovely late summer and autumn flowers for sunny positions. My favourite is the hybrid 'Autumn Joy', whose large salmon-pink flower heads on 2ft (60cm) stems are impossible to ignore in any garden in September and October. As they age, the blooms deepen to shades of red and reddish-brown. This splendid plant is a cross between *S. spectabile* and *S. telephium*.

Another sedum of real quality is the *S. spectabile* variety 'Brilliant' which bears deep rose flowers on 1½ft (45cm) stems at the same time as 'Autumn Joy'. You can achieve some very good effects also by planting on the edge of a bed the cream-variegated *S. telephium variegatum*.

The same kind of warm, sunny sheltered conditions are needed by the *Agapanthus* Headbourne Hybrids, splendid plants for July-August flowering, and much hardier that the other agapanthuses, or African lilies as they are called. Even so, they are not plants for really cold gardens, and if the situation is borderline it is certainly worth protecting the crowns of the plants with a covering of dry litter or well-weathered ashes in winter. These hybrids are 2 to 4ft (60cm to 1.3m) in height, have bold, strap-shaped leaves of rich green colouring and throw up a wealth of highly decorative umbels of pale blue to violet-blue flowers on strong stems. As I've mentioned in the chapter on plants for containers, they are excellent for growing in tubs or other large, deep containers. In the garden they grow well in any ordinary, well-drained soil.

Provide just the same congenial conditions suggested for the agapanthuses for that lovely rhizomatous perennial from South Africa, *Schizostylis coccinea*, or one of its varieties like 'Major' (which has red, star-flowers like the species but of larger size) or the pale pink 'Mrs Hegarty'. Any one of these can be a lovely sight from late September to November when the delicate spikes of small flowers are borne on 2ft (60cm) stems above grass-like foliage – but they are not plants to even attempt to grow in a cold garden. You should plant the rhizomes in spring to get them off to a good start and give the roots a covering of dry litter in winter.

We have been able to enjoy for quite a few years now a range of

Paeonia *'Bowl of Beauty'*

Rudbeckia fulgida
'Goldsturm' (see p. 104).

*A pink form of* Schizostylis
coccinea *provides welcome
colour from late September to
November (see p. 105).*

phormiums with attractive 'architectural', evergreen foliage. Mostly, these are cultivars, bred in New Zealand, of the well-known 8 to 10ft (2.5 to 3m) tall New Zealand flax, *Phormium tenax*, which has been grown in the more climatically favoured gardens of Britain for not far short of two hundred years, but a few are derivatives of the smaller-growing *P. cookianum*, a species which has been grown here for over one hundred years

The foliage of these plants is sword-shaped and mostly two-toned, so that they have quite a lot to offer as decorative features for the patio garden, whether grown in warm, sheltered borders or in containers, for which purpose they are admirably suited (indeed, grown in that way they can be taken under cover during winter to avoid any risk of weather damage). What they must have to succeed is good soil, good drainage and exposure to plenty of sunshine

The tallest of these varieties and hybrids is around 6ft (2m) tall (*P. tenax* 'Purpureum', which has purplish leaves, as the name suggests), but the majority of them are 2 to 3ft (60cm to 1m) tall. They include 'Maori Sunrise', with pinkish, apricot and bronze-margined leaves; 'Dazzler', reddish-brown, banded with carmine-red; 'Sundowner', greyish-purple, margined with creamy-pink; and Yellow Wave', golden-yellow, edged green.

They do not take too kindly to extreme cold and they should always be given a warm, sheltered position such as can so often be provided in patio garden conditions. For the first winter at least give them protection against frost in the form of a 4in (10cm) layer of bracken, leaves or straw. Container-grown specimens, as I've already said, can be kept in a frost-proof place over-winter. I favour this method of cultivation.

There is another side also to the phormium story. If you already take an interest in phormiums generally you will know that they are as likely to be found listed in the shrub section of nurserymen's catalogues as in the perennial-plant section; like-wise in gardening books. As non-woody plants they are true perennials, but it is interesting to note that on the finer points of their taxonomy the botanists also find it difficult to make up their minds. Phormiums have recently been removed from the *Liliaceae* (or lily) family and put into the *Agavaceae* (or agave) family; but this, one gathers, may not yet be the last word on the subject. No wonder we gardeners get confused at times!

Of course, I have no more than scratched the surface of the rich array of herbaceous perennial plants on offer by nurserymen, many of them highly suitable for small set-piece plantings in patio gardens. What I have done, I hope, is to point the way to some of those most deserving of a place in a patio garden, where every inch of space is precious.

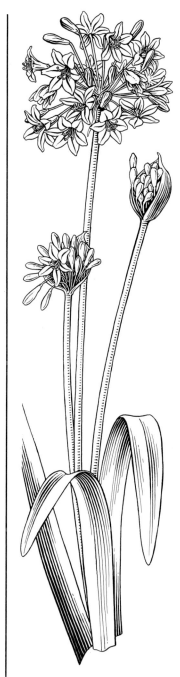

Agapanthus *Headbourne Hybrids (see p. 105).*

# 7. The Patio Pool

Given that you can find a nice sunny spot for it – sunshine is a necessity – a small pool can add greatly to the attractions of a patio garden. It gives the garden an air of peace and tranquillity, whether it is the still water reflecting the clouds and sky or, say, the soft babblings of a small fountain on a still summer's day. All in all, it provides beauty and interest out of all proportion to its size.

But what kind of pool? There is no reason at all why you should not have a concrete one provided you have the ability to make this really well or are prepared to go to the expense of having it made professionally so that it will be leak-proof and will not readily be breached by arctic weather. To make sure of that the concrete must be at least 5in (13cm) thick and be treated with a waterproofing preparation.

It is altogether easier though, these days, to opt for a glass-fibre pool or to use a heavy-duty plastic pool liner for which you have but to prepare a hole of the right size and shape. Certainly you have got to take care when making the preparations, for it is important when seating glass-fibre pools that the support should be even all round. If you leave loose pockets of soil around the sides the weight of the water pressing on the frame is liable to cause strain and distortion.

With the plastic pool liner the important thing is to make sure that no sharp stones are left sticking through the soil when the hole has been excavated. If you don't, then the weight of the water pressing down on sharp edges will be liable to cause tears. Lining the hole with a layer of sand before putting down the liner should ensure that this does not happen.

A pool made from either of these two materials can be effectively camouflaged with an edging of paving stones. Useful as these materials are, one does not want to be too conscious of their presence.

### Planting the pool
When it comes to planting the garden pool, too, do remember the cardinal rule about design in general: keep it simple. Don't attempt to pack in too many plants. Water-lilies (nymphaeas), which everybody wants to grow, are certainly not seen to best advantage if overcrowded, nor do they grow so well.

Let us start with water-lilies, as these are so popular. It is important to make sure that those you choose are suitable for the depth of water you can provide; and if you have a small pool – which is certainly what I would consider right for a typical patio garden – keep away from those which are too vigorous or wide-spreading.

Choose, for instance, something like the splendid 'James Brydon', a cultivar with rosy-red blooms which makes much less foliage than some others and will happily grow in anything from 7in to 2ft (18 to 60cm) of water. The yellow *Nymphaea pygmaea* 'Helvola' will grow well in as little as 6in (15cm) of water, while two for a minimum depth of 9in (23cm) are the soft pink 'Laydekeri Lilacea', which matures to rosy-red, and the rosy-crimson 'Laydekeri Purpurata'. In the same depth of water you can grow the deep red 'Froebelii' and the handsome pink 'Rose Arey'. Many others are readily available.

It is more usual nowadays to plant water-lilies in polythene containers than in prepared beds of soil on the base of the pool. It is easier this way, and the growing medium, which should consist of a rather heavy soil, is more effectively contained. If you do plant directly into a bed of soil on the base of the pool, however, this soil can be confined by a ring of stones. You can dress the soil too at planting time with a proprietary water-lily fertiliser, obtainable from garden stores.

Still, water-lilies, lovely as they are, are not the be-all and end-all of water gardening. The double marsh marigold, *Caltha palustris plena*, for instance, brings a fine splash of gold to the garden in spring. Another distinctive plant for display just a little later is the golden club, *Orontium aquaticum*. The common name is apt for the yellow flowers, individually very small, clothe the upper part of the white stems which are thrown up in spring. Then for early summer what could be better than the water iris, *Iris laevigata*, with its beautiful blue flowers on 2ft (60cm) stems; or, for late summer or early autumn display, than the pale blue-flowered *Pontederia cordata*, a plant with heart-shaped leaves. All these are suitable for shallow water, say around 3in (8cm) deep,

Nymphaea *'Rose Arey'*

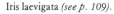
Iris laevigata *(see p. 109)*.

but the caltha will be happy only in water 1in (3cm) deep and the orontium in water from 3 to 18in (8 to 45cm) deep.

The best planting months for aquatics are May and June with planting continuing until early August. Keep this fact in mind when you are laying your plans.

### Fish and fountains

If you introduce fish like goldfish, golden orfe or shubunkins to the pool, and it is pleasant to see them darting here and there, then submerged oxygenating plants like the water violet,

*Hottonia palustris*, a plant which puts up to the surface stems bearing pretty lilac-coloured flowers in early summer, are a necessity to keep the water clear and sweet. Another good plant for this purpose is the water starwort, *Callitriche verna*.

A fountain can be operated by a submersible or external pump, electrically powered. Underwater lighting kits, complete with low-voltage transformers, add a new dimension of interest to a water feature, and have a special attraction in a patio garden where you will want to sit out on summer evenings. A very pleasing prospect.

# 8. Plants in Containers

There is no need to stress the value of plants grown in tubs, window-boxes and containers of other kinds in the context of the patio garden, and the smaller patio area the greater part they have to play. Large containers, too, can be used for permanent plantings of climbers and shrubs, if they are treated as I suggest later (see p. 122).

### Choice of compost
This kind of gardening is immensely enjoyable and rewarding, but like everything else it imposes its own set of rules and disciplines. It is necessary to appreciate right from the start that if you are going to confine plants in such close quarters it is essential to provide them with good fare. Old worn-out soil from the garden just is not good enough.

So what should it be? The choice is quite wide: the John Innes potting composts (Nos. 1, 2 and 3), proprietary soilless mixtures and composts which you can make up yourself.

Let us look at each in turn. I make much use of the soilless, peat-based composts but to fill a large container with one of these costs quite a lot of money, as indeed it does if the John Innes composts are used. Of these two types the John Innes are a better choice for shrubs and larger plants generally of a permanent nature as they provide more support for the plants in windy weather and do not need the regular feeding which is essential with soilless composts, after the initial food content of the compost has been used up. It is important to appreciate that with soilless composts a complete fertiliser including trace elements must be used as directed by the manufacturer.

If you use John Innes composts, however, pay proper attention to the grade you use for these vary in their fertiliser content. So, it should be No. 1 grade for plants which are of a transient nature; No. 2 for what might be termed semi-permanent plants, and No. 3 for long-term occupants of containers, bearing in mind that very small plants should not be introduced to the No. 3 grade until they have grown larger.

As John Innes composts contain ground chalk they should not be used for lime-hating plants like rhododendrons, azaleas and camellias. The same applies to the loamless composts, of course, and in both types of compost (soil-based and soilless) there are lime-free versions – termed ericaceous mixtures – available. Alternatively, use a mixture consisting of lime-free loam to which liberal quantities of peat and sand have been added.

I mentioned home-made mixtures. It is possible to buy proprietary compost-making kits which allow you to make up your own soilless, peat-based composts to a given formula, or rather any one of numerous formulas for a wide range of purposes. For those prepared to go to the trouble involved in making up such mixtures there are definite cost advantages. Quite different again is a method of compost-making for permanent container plants like shrubs, and indeed, for shorter-term plants like bulbous flowers and summer bedders, which I have found completely satisfactory over the past two to three years. This is to mix equal quantities of composted bark (available from garden centres and stores) with good garden loam. Naturally, I feed the plants with liquid fertiliser, as necessary.

**Points to remember**
Drainage must be good for any container-grown plant so the container must have an adequate number of holes in its base for drainage, with a layer of porous material between this and the growing compost. With the dominance of plastic pots and containers nowadays over their clay equivalents crocks are hard to come by but pebbles and small stones are good substitutes. Cover these in turn with rough-textured material from the compost heap or elsewhee to stop the compost filtering through.

Make sure, too, that the container's base is raised off the ground so that excess moisture can drain away freely. With window-boxes, of course, it is the wall fittings or brackets which must be strong enough to do their job properly. A box laden with soil and plants can be surprisingly heavy and can be a menace if not properly secured.

Which brings me to another point. One of the plus factors with containers is their mobility, but if you think you are going to do a lot of scene shifting with the seasons you may be in for a disappointment. If a window-box or large pot can be heavy that is nothing to a typical garden tub or concrete plant container with all its impedimenta. It is usually more than a single-handed job, which means that in practice you leave them alone as much as possible.

With container plants – and even more with hanging baskets – you must be constantly aware of their need for water. On a hot summer day, with the sun beating down, the compost can dry out in next to no time. So try to get a neighbour or a friend to give them a drink in such weather even if you have to be away yourself.

*Tulipa kaufmanniana*

## Bulbs

A wide range of plants can be used for window-box display and for growing in other containers to give vibrant colour for many months of the year – from bulbous flowers early on to annuals like the showy marigolds, antirrhinums, nasturtiums and the like later in the season.

Bulbs can make a heart-warming show in spring for a quite modest expenditure weighed against the pleasure they give. For example, such strong-growing trumpet daffodil varieties as 'Golden Harvest' and 'King Alfred' will put up an impressive show from plantings made in September or October, setting the bulbs 4in (10cm) deep. The beautiful water-lily tulips, too, the varieties and hybrids of *Tulipa kaufmanniana*, are ideal for container gardening, providing brilliant colour in March and April; some of the hybrids also have the most exquisitely marked foliage as a result of crossing *T. kaufmanniana* with *T. greigii*. These hybrids are anything from 4in to 10in (10 to 25cm) tall.

Other tulips you could grow would be the lovely varieties and hybrids of *T. fosteriana*, at least the shorter ones (they range in height from 9in to 18in (23 to 45cm), and certain of the *T. greigii* kinds like the scarlet, black and bronze 'Red Riding Hood' and the richly coloured 'Cape Cod' (bronze-yellow and black with bold red stripes on the outside of the petals), which do not make so much height as the others. Find them a nice sunny position and plant the bulbs 4in (10cm) deep and 6in (15cm) apart an any time between September and November.

You can do the same also with the Double Earlies, which are very attractive. For all, it is essential that the compost should be well drained.

What else? Well, of course, hyacinths are delightful for flowering in late March and early April, and these you plant in September or October, 4in (10cm) deep; also snowdrops, which you plant at the same time and at the same depth. Either *Galanthus nivalis*, the common snowdrop, or *G. elwesii* will put up a splendid show early in the year.

The Siberian squill, *Scilla sibirica*, muscari (grape hyacinths) in variety, dwarf irises like the beautiful little *Iris reticulata* which flowers in February and March, and a whole range of dwarf narcissi and crocuses can be pressed into service to provide a display. These last all need planting about 3in (8cm) deep in September or October.

Just a mention, too, of the regal lily, *Lilium regale*, more fully described on p. 132, which makes a splendid tub plant for providing colour in July. Its trumpet flowers are white, flushed yellow in the throat and rose-purple on the outside of the petals. It needs a sunny position.

For all of these you could use one of the compost mixtures I have suggested for general use (p. 112), but if the bulbs are

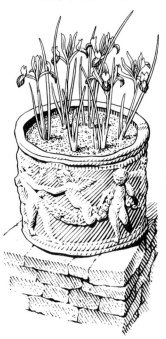

Iris reticulata *(see p. 114)*.

replacing plants which have been giving a summer display do not bother to bring in fresh compost. The same mixture will be quite adequate, provided it is of an open texture so that the drainage is beyond reproach. If necessary, take the old compost out and mix in with it some peat and sharp sand.

Watch the watering as well and make sure that at no time is the compost allowed to become dry.

### Bedding plants

There is nothing like the joy of seeing spring flowers, especially on those days – and we do get them – when the weather is warm enough to sit among them and take in their beauty in a contemplative way. All the same, it is the summer bedding plants, either raised oneself if the facilities are available or bought in as young plants, which are the really significant plants for use in containers on the patio, as they are for small beds, if the design allows for such display. A whole host of lovely things can be used to good effect, from impatiens (busy lizzies) and petunias to calendulas and tagetes (marigolds) to nasturtiums, ageratums and smaller-growing antirrhinums to celosias (cockscombs), salvias, dwarf varieties of *Begonia semperflorens, Phlox drummondii* varieties, China asters (callistephuses) and other plants raised from seed.

If you buy boxes of these make quite sure that the roots of the plants are thoroughly moistened before planting, for if you don't you will find that is extremely difficult to get the dry root balls to take up moisture later. What usually happens is that the plant remains dry while the new compost gets over-moist and in extreme cases becomes sour – a very unsatisfactory state of affairs.

### Shrubs and sub-shrubs

Clematis are marvellous patio plants whether grown in beds or in containers. The early, large-flowered hybrids (which I discussed on p. 28) are wonderfully convenient, easy and successful climbers to grow in tubs or other large containers made of wood or stone. Likewise the cultivars of *Clematis alpina* and *C. macropetala* (see p. 28). These last two types also look extremely attractive grown in old strawberry pots. The *C. montana* cultivars are really a little too vigorous for container cultivation, and that is true also of the mid-season flowering hybrids like 'Marie Boisselot', the 'Jackmanii' types and the later flowering species. The role of these highly decorative kinds lies elsewhere, as indicated earlier (p. 29).

The zonal and ivy-leaved pelargoniums (or geraniums) are, of course, indispensible container plants, like the hortensia cultivars of the common hydrangea, *H. macrophylla*, and the fuchsias which are available in such variety.

It is well known, of course, that the colour of the flowers of

*A hortensia hydrangea.*

hortensia hydrangeas is directly related to the chemical composition of the soil. You don't get blue shades on alkaline, or limy, soils but shades of pink and red. In such circumstances you can, of course, apply a proprietary blueing agent if you so desire. One of my favourite varieties is the splendid 'Génerale Vicomtesse de Vibraye', for it is notably generous in producing its blooms – either a lovely clear blue or rose-pink, depending on the soil you grow it in. Other excellent varieties include the deep rose-pink or deep blue 'Hamburg', the deep pink or purplish-blue 'Maréchal Foch', and the superb 'Madame E. Mouillière', white. You could also make a very nice show with the hybrid 'Preziosa' grown in this way. It is described on p. 49.

These hydrangeas can be grown in sunshine or light shade, like fuchsias. Of the latter there are also many varieties from which to make a choice, among them excellent ones like the dwarf cerise and mauve 'Tom Thumb', the white, pink and violet-mauve 'Chillerton Beauty' and 'Mrs Popple', a very good performer with scarlet and purple flowers.

At the end of the season you can store your container-grown hydrangeas and fuchsias in any cool, frost-proof place like the

**Opposite:** *Fuchsias and pelargoniums provide a riot of late-season colour.*

**Left:** Hedera helix *'Buttercup' – one of the most effective of all the ivies.*

*Azalea (see p. 120).*

garage, until the warmer weather returns. Pelargoniums need overwintering in good light and frost-proof conditions.

Of course, if you have little space to grow plants in beds, and that is quite often the case in the small patio garden, you can grow all manner of things successfully in containers, provided they are large enough. Shrubs like the evergreen azaleas and Japanese maples (cultivars of *Acer palmatum*), the cheery yellow-flowered winter jasmine (*Jasminium nudiflorum*) and *Forsythia intermedia spectabilis* or the excellent 'Lynwood' are a natural choice, not to mention ornamental vines like the Virginia creeper (*Parthenocissus quinquefolia*); ivies like the variegated Persian type, *Hedera colchica* 'Dentata Variegata', and the splendid *H. helix* 'Buttercup'; the beautiful camellias, lovely in leaf alone even when they are not

Viburnum davidii

Pinus mugo pumilio

carrying their exotic-looking flowers, roses and clematises. There are numerous others, like the bold-leaved *Fatsia japonica* (see p. 62), the bay laurel, *Laurus nobilis* (so long as its site does not subject it to severe cold), and the very handsome-foliaged, small-growing variety of the common laurel, *Prunus laurocerasus* 'Otto Luyken'. This has small, narrow leaves which are dark green and shiny and it makes a wide-spreading shrub about 3 to 4ft (1 to 1.3m) tall. It bears spikes of white flowers in May.

I must put in a word, too, for the charming little variegated evergreen *Euonymus fortunei* 'Silver Queen', which, free-standing in a tub or a bed, will remain small and spreading – not more than 2ft (60cm) tall – but which up against a wall will climb to a height of about 10ft (3m). The small leaves are margined with creamy-white and it is an attraction at all seasons. Then there is that recently introduced foliage plant, the evergreen *Euonymus fortunei* 'Emerald 'n' Gold', about 1ft (30cm) high, which clothes itself in bright yellow and green leaves slightly tinged with pink (in the garden it is an excellent ground cover).

Also excellent for container growing are *Berberis stenophylla* 'Corallina Compacta', *Elaeagnus pungens* 'Maculata', *Viburnum davidii* and *Daphne odora* 'Aureomarginata', all of which I have discussed in the chapter on shrubs (see pp. 23 to 64 and index).

Of the above, though, do note that the evergreen azaleas and camellias demand a lime-free soil. Make a special note too, of the following azaleas, for they are especially attractive: 'Hinodegiri', bright crimson, 'Vuyk's Scarlet', the pure white 'Palestrina' and the salmon-pink 'Blaauw's Pink', all of which make modestly sized shrubs and flower in May. A sheltered, very lightly shaded position suits them best of all but they will grow well in sun if need be.

**Dwarf conifers**
Don't overlook either the value of dwarf and slow-growing conifers as tub specimens, for the foliage can provide year-round interest with its colour and texture. A conifer which is often grown in this way is *Chamaecyparis lawsoniana* 'Ellwoodii', columnar in habit and grey-green foliaged, but a rather better choice might be the form known as *C. lawsoniana* 'Ellwood's Gold' (see p. 78), in that the yellow tips to the growths give it a more lively appearance. For this coloration to be good, though, it needs to be placed in a sunny position.

Another *lawsoniana* variety to consider is the small, globular *C. lawsoniana* 'Minima Glauca', little over 2ft (60cm) tall, which has sea-green foliage and is very slow to put on growth, which is no disadvantage in a container plant.

I'm very fond of the dwarf form of the mountain pine, *Pinus mugo pumilio*, another conifer which can be used very satisfactorily for this purpose with its mass of dark green, tufty, spreading growths. It has a lot of character and is unlikely to be more than 3ft (1m) tall grown in this way. The ultra-slow growing *Juniperus communis* 'Compressa' is, of course, the one used so often in sink gardens, and very attractive it is making its conical mat of growth and eventually reaching, after years, a height of perhaps 2ft (60cm). Another juniper to consider is the distinctive *J. media* 'Blaauw', which makes a quite sizeable specimen with upward-thrusting branches which arch over at the top. Its foliage colour is greyish-green. There are, of course, numerous others which can be grown in this way.

What has given me great pleasure over the past two years is a collection of dwarf and slow-growing conifers which I am growing in clay pots of various sizes, some of small size. There are over 40 of them all together, all of different kinds, and it is amazing how much interest these provide at every season. Moreover, they take up very little room, a point of importance if such a collection is made in a corner of a patio garden – something I would recommend.

Mine include the three just referred to, namely *Pinus mugo pumilio*, *Chamaecyparis lawsoniana* 'Minima Glauca' and *Juniperus communis* 'Compressa', and other attractive plants like the prostrate-growing *Microcachrys tetragona* which bears showy little red cones from autumn onwards throughout the winter; *Chamaecyparis lawsoniana* 'Pygmaea Argentea', the foliage tips of which are creamy-white; *Picea abies* 'Gregoryana', which makes a rounded bush, eventually of 1 to 1½ft (30 to 45cm) in height, with light green foliage in spring which contrasts with the darker, older foliage; the very small growing *Thuja occidentalis* 'Hetz Midget' and the very dwarf *Cedrus libani* 'Nana'. All are very distinctive and fascinating to observe over a period of time.

I grow all of these conifers in John Innes No. 2 potting compost, replacing a little of the surface compost in the spring with fresh compost of like kind – and taking care, of course, not to disturb the roots in the process. The plants are also given a light dressing of bone-meal in spring. No other feeding is necessary or desirable.

Be very careful to water the plants correctly. Conifers grown in pots will almost certainly need daily watering in summer (so make arrangements for this when you are going on holiday) except in dull, rainy weather, but between October and spring only water when this is really necessary. To let conifers dry right out is likely to lead to disaster, for plants allowed to suffer in this way rarely recover.

Specialist nurseries offer the conifers I have referred to, and many others as well.

Note that the interesting new range of phormiums (ornamented flaxes) which I have discussed in the chapter on perennials (see p. 107) are highly suited for container cultivation. Their clearly

*Juniperus media 'Blaauw'*

**Above:** *A dwarf broom and pine,* Bellis perennis *(daisy) and violas make a charming container planting.*

**Opposite:** *This hanging basket and vase planting gives the scene an almost Mediterranean air.*

defined 'architectural' forms and colourings could add much to the attractions of a paved area (see illustration on p. 18). The *Agapanthus* Headbourne Hybrids, described on p. 105, are also excellent plants for growing in tubs or other large, deep containers.

There is advice on growing strawberries in containers on p.168.

### Care of plants in containers

Whatever permanent plants you grow in containers, though, you must take the trouble to see that they are provided with the optimum growing conditions. This means really efficient drainage, the right kind of compost, sunshine or shade as the case may be. Attend to their watering needs, too, with particular assiduity for containers can dry out remarkably quickly in hot, sunny weather, a point already noted in relation to pot-grown conifers.

Make it a matter of routine, too, to give such permanent plants a top-dressing of new compost each spring, again just as suggested for conifers in pots. Remove with great care the top few inches of old soil – or as much as you can without disturbing the roots of the plants – and replace this with new compost which you firm in place with your fingers. This always gives the plants a

Sometimes a new house or a conversion of an old house opens on to a garden area enclosed by walls on at least two sides. The area represented here is about 60ft (18m) across by 40ft (12m) deep, and the design exploits the intimate atmosphere already partly provided by the end of an adjoining property and the wall which abuts on to it. Slight changes of level provide additional interest and it should be noted that such a feature, with raised beds, can have practical advantages as well if the soil is heavy and the drainage none too good.

The panel of grass on the left increases the usable sitting-out space in summer and its greenness can be very welcome in winter, when muted tones predominate.

Note, also, how the two small trees give the garden a sense of balance with the shrubs, the tall conifer and the climbers on the far wall breaking up what would otherwise be a hard line which, inevitably, would jar on the senses. With relative ease a site like this can be transformed into a patio garden of considerable charm.

new lease of life. It is usually necessary to feed container-grown shrubs in the growing season as well for they cannot fend for themselves in a similar way to those grown in the open ground. There are numerous proprietary liquid feeds available.

## Hanging baskets

Another type of container display which can give added charm to the patio garden in summer is to have flower-filled hanging baskets dotted around, perhaps hung on brackets near a door into the house or attached to some other wall or fence. They can indeed be great fun and immensely colourful if you use plants like ivy-leaved pelargoniums (geraniums), blue-flowered trailing lobelia and verbena, petunias and nasturtiums. Here again, too, fuchsias come into their own and tuberous and fibrous-rooted begonias.

Once again, though, I would advise taking more than usual care in the preparation of the baskets and watch especially the subsequent watering. On a very hot summer's day the baskets need, ideally, several soakings, but for busy people away from home all day I realise that that may be a counsel of perfection. What I do say is that you should make a thorough job of watering, the best way being by immersing the basket in a container for perhaps 10 minutes or so but otherwise doing this in the ordinary way with a watering can. As with other container-grown plants, also give the plants a liquid feed at regular intervals in summer. Once a fortnight is not too often for the plants really are in very confined conditions.

Preparing a hanging basket is simple enough. First line the basket with well-moistened sphagnum moss or plastic sheeting, then add compost and firm it well with the fingers. Plant the trailing plants around the sides first (if plastic sheeting is used, making slits in this for planting) and then put in the rest of the plants so that you end up by filling the last bare space in the centre of the basket. Water thoroughly with a watering can (not by immersion until the compost has had a chance to settle down) and all is then ready to hang the basket in position.

If you try your hand at the kind of container gardening I have been suggesting, I shall be very surprised if you do not find it immensely rewarding. Try experimenting with all kinds of plants – for that is half the fun of gardening – and gradually find out what is most suitable for your patio.

*Baskets of flowers can add much interest to a patio garden.*

# 9. Colourful Bulbs

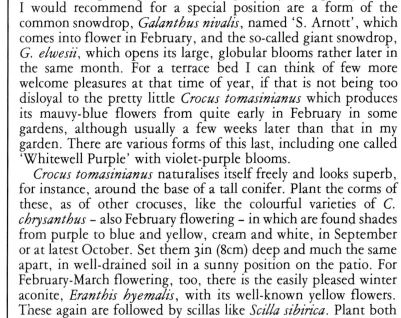

Opposite: *Snowdrops (galanthus) in all their wide diversity are a great joy early in the year.*

In the last chapter, I mentioned some bulbous plants which are excellent for growing in containers. Of course, all can be grown with equal or greater effect in beds if the space can be found.

### Early flowering bulbs
Two snowdrops of quite outstanding beauty and quality which I would recommend for a special position are a form of the common snowdrop, *Galanthus nivalis*, named 'S. Arnott', which comes into flower in February, and the so-called giant snowdrop, *G. elwesii*, which opens its large, globular blooms rather later in the same month. For a terrace bed I can think of few more welcome pleasures at that time of year, if that is not being too disloyal to the pretty little *Crocus tomasinianus* which produces its mauvy-blue flowers from quite early in February in some gardens, although usually a few weeks later than that in my garden. There are various forms of this last, including one called 'Whitewell Purple' with violet-purple blooms.

    *Crocus tomasinianus* naturalises itself freely and looks superb, for instance, around the base of a tall conifer. Plant the corms of these, as of other crocuses, like the colourful varieties of *C. chrysanthus* – also February flowering – in which are found shades from purple to blue and yellow, cream and white, in September or at latest October. Set them 3in (8cm) deep and much the same apart, in well-drained soil in a sunny position on the patio. For February-March flowering, too, there is the easily pleased winter aconite, *Eranthis hyemalis*, with its well-known yellow flowers. These again are followed by scillas like *Scilla sibirica*. Plant both 2in (5cm) deep in September or October.

### Bulbs for spring
What would spring be like without the daffodils in their multitudinous forms? A much duller season, without a doubt. A whole host of the larger kinds from the trumpet varieties to the large- and small-cupped kinds and the doubles can be put to good use in the patio garden, growing around shrubs and roses and in other situations where their early colour will be appreciated. They like good soil but will put up with very mediocre concoctions if need be. On poorer soils it is well worth lacing the

Crocus tomasinianus

Narcissus *'February Gold'*

Narcissus cyclamineus

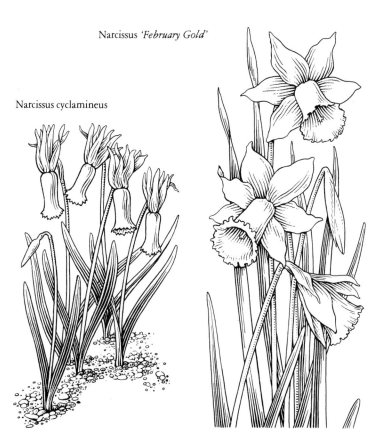

planting area with bone-meal at the rate of 4oz (113g) to the square yard when the soil is being prepared. Plant the bulbs in August or as soon thereafter as practicable, setting them 4 to 6in (10 to 15cm) deep, the greater depth on light soils.

But it is the exquisite little dwarf narcissi which really capture one's heart, and these are ideal for patio garden conditions. Particularly lovely is the February-March flowering *Narcissus cyclamineus* and its offspring. Many very attractive garden hybrids have been obtained by crossing this species with trumpet varieties. The species itself has reflexed perianth segments resembling those of a cyclamen – hence the name – and the narrow trumpet combines with these to make a flower of great charm. To be grown well, though, it needs rather a moist soil which contains plenty of humus. The hybrids I've just referred to include varieties like 'February Gold', 'March Sunshine', 'Peeping Tom', 'Dove Wings', 'Jenny' and 'Charity May'. All are excellent and they are nearly all 10 to 12in (25 to 30cm) tall, with 'Peeping Tom' being one of those which has a height of up to 15in (38cm).

Then there is the beautiful hoop petticoat daffodil, *N. bulbocodium*, with is distinctive, flared, trumpet-shaped yellow blooms which appear in February and March as well.

For April flowering there are the crosses between *N. triandrus* and *N. jonquilla* with names like 'April Tears', 'Hawera' and 'Rippling Waters'. The first two are about 9in (23cm) tall and very pretty with, in the case of 'April Tears', up to five deep yellow flowers to a stem, rather less in the case of the lemon-yellow 'Hawera'. 'Rippling Waters' has three pure white, cup-shaped blooms to a stem. The bulbs of all these small narcissi should also be planted in August or as soon thereafter as possible, but only 2 to 3in (6 to 8cm) deep, the greater depth being in light soil.

Of course, one of the most popular small bulbous plants is the muscari (or grape hyacinth) in its various species and forms. Nothing could be more accommodating, either, for it will grow happily in sunshine or light shade in almost any reasonable soil. Grown with daffodils, as in the raised beds which so often form a part of a paved patio area, they can be a delight in April – and none more so than the well-known *Muscari armeniacum* 'Heavenly Blue', some 6in (15cm) tall and with flowers of a vivid blue. An interesting, rather earlier flowering species is *M. tuberginianum* 8in (20cm) tall which got its name of Oxford and Cambridge grape hyacinth from its way of bearing dark blue flowers at the top of the spike, pale blue ones lower down. It is often in flower before March is out. Plant the bulbs 3in (8cm) deep between late August and early November, but preferably as early as possible.

More, too, about the scillas which I mentioned earlier in passing. These also are easy-going little plants, but they will always do best where there is plenty of moisture in the soil combined with free drainage. Sunshine or light shade suits them equally well. One of the best for brightening March days is the 6in (15cm) *Scilla sibirica atrocoerulea*, or 'Spring Beauty' as it is often called. For ordinary garden conditions it is the best one to grow.

Of course, the other very popular group of bulbous plants is the tulips, to which I have already made reference in respect of the species and their varieties and hybrids (see p. 114). How pleasant also to find a home for some of the colourful bedding kinds, allowing that these should be lifted and the bulbs stored in a cool, dry place after the foliage has died down in summer until planting time comes round once more. The planting time for these tulips is in October and November and you set the bulbs between 4 and 5in (10 to 13cm) deep, the lighter the soil the deeper the planting. What they need, too, is an especially well-drained soil, in sun or light shade.

Before looking at some of the bedding kinds, though, I must sing the praises of some of the species and their hybrids for special parts of the garden, and it should be noted that these do not need lifting every season, like the bedding kinds. For example, the *T. kaufmanniana* varieties and hybrids, which I have recommended

Scilla sibirica
atrocoerulea

129

Tulipa kaufmanniana
'Gluck', one of the numerous
hybrids of this species, which
can be associated most
beautifully with bedding plants
like polyanthus.

Lilium candidum

for container growing, look quite magnificent in a bed set in paving, and these together with the *T. fosteriana* hybrids and the *T. greigii* hybrids – these last flower from late April – are splendid for a raised bed. Even a few make a striking display. Note, however, that tulips of this type need planting in a sunny position and the bulbs need planting some 4in (10cm) deep.

To go back to the bedding tulips, take special note of the single early and double early kinds which are around 1ft (30cm) tall and make a striking display in the second half of April, and of the spectacular Darwin hybrids which flower from late April and are unsurpassed for a formal display in a small bed set in paving. These have single blooms on 2ft (60cm) stems. Just a few May-flowering lily-flowered tulips are also a joy for these have a grace which demands attention.

Hyacinths can be planted in beds and make a colourful display in spring and these you should plant 4in (10cm) deep between September and November. They like a good soil and excellent drainage and you should lift the bulbs in summer when the foliage has withered and store – after removing the remains of the foliage – in a cool, airy place until planting time arrives again.

If part of your patio is lightly shaded and the soil there is nicely moisture-retentive then you might think of growing one of my favourite bulbs, the so-called summer snowflake, *Leucojum aestivum*, which, despite its common name, flowers in April and May. It is a very elegant plant with its white, bell-shaped flowers with green markings on the tips of the petals, these being borne in nodding umbels on stems some 2ft (60cm) tall. In some ways this plant looks like an outsize snowdrop. The strong foliage is strap-shaped and makes the perfect foil for the flowers. But get the form 'Gravetye Variety', which is even better than the species. Plant the bulbs in September or October 4in (10cm) deep. This plant increases freely and should be left alone until the quality of the blooms starts dropping off. Then lift, divide and replant the bulbs after flowering has finished and the foliage has died back.

## Lilies

I am going to mention only a couple of lilies although there are rich pickings here for anybody keen on this beautiful genus. First, the very popular regal lily, *Lilium regale*, which makes a superb tub plant and a first-class border plant as well for it grows well in practically all soils – it does not mind lime – provided they are well drained. The white trumpet flowers, carried in bold heads on 4 to 6ft (1.3 to 2m) stems in July, have yellow throat markings and rosy-purple suffusions on the outside of the petals. What it does need is plenty of sunshine, and you should plant the bulbs in autumn as soon as these can be obtained from the supplier for no lily bulb improves by being out of the ground for long.

The regal lily is stem rooting so the bulbs should be set 8 to 10in (20 to 25cm) deep in the soil and, like all lilies, be bedded in sharp sand at the base of the planting hole to avoid the possibility of rotting in wet weather.

The other lily is *L. candidum*, the Madonna lily, with a history which goes back into the mists of time. Indeed, its glorious white, broad-petalled blooms set off by golden-yellow anthers have been enjoyed in Britain for centuries, and this species from the eastern Mediterranean was reproduced on pottery by Cretan craftsmen before 1500 B.C. Ten or more flower heads are borne on each 4 to 5ft (1.3 to 1.5m) stem in June and July, sometimes as many as 20 flowers, but that is still well below the maximum you can get in the inflorescence of *L. regale*.

This also is a lily which does not mind lime in the soil, and the conditions it needs are similar to those liked by *L. regale*, a well-drained soil, of reasonable quality, warmth and sunshine, but its planting regime is different – indeed it is different from that of almost every other lily. It needs to be planted in July or August, just as soon as the bulbs can be obtained. Also untypically they need to be planted only 1in (2.5cm) deep. This lily is subject to attack by botrytis, in hot, airless weather and as soon as this is noticed the plants should be sprayed with Bordeaux mixture. Have no hesitation though in lifting and burning any really badly attacked plants.

### Sternbergia and nerine

Another sun-loving bulbous plant is *Sternbergia lutea*, which produces in September and October attractive crocus-like flowers above strap-shaped leaves. A well-drained bed at the foot of a warm wall is ideal for this plant and it appreciates good soil. The sheltered conditions found in the typical patio garden are the kind of home it likes. Leave the bulbs undisturbed until the quality of the flowers starts to drop off and then lift and divide in July or August, the time when you buy the plant bulbs when starting off. Plant the bulbs 4in (10cm) deep.

*Sternbergia lutea* is not all that well known, and it does need a warm spot, so you may have been wondering why I haven't mentioned the autumn crocus, *Colchicum autumnale*, and its forms which put on a show at the same time of year. I'm fond of them in fact, but one cannot overlook the obtrusiveness of the large leaves from early spring to mid-summer in the confines of a small garden. Still, there are the very gay autumn crocuses proper, the varieties of *Crocus speciosus*, with their very good colour range. These are suitable for sunny positions.

I am going to leave the bulbs with a mention of a barely hardy plant of great beauty, *Nerine bowdenii*, which needs very similar conditions to the sternbergia just referred to, and a good loamy soil with excellent drainage. If you can find a sheltered spot for it

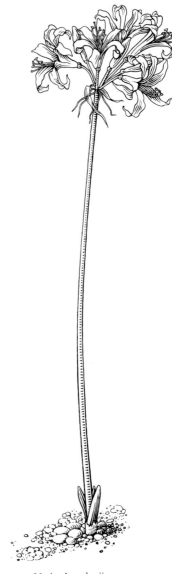

Nerine bowdenii

at the foot of a sheltered, south-facing wall that would be ideal. The flowers are borne in umbels of six or more on 2ft (60cm) stems, each flower consisting of narrow, reflexed segments in pale pink colouring with a darker line down the centre. The strap-like leaves do not usually arrive until after the flowers, which are there to be enjoyed from late September until

*The regal lily*, Lilium regale, *rightly popular with its beautiful flowers which are borne in July (see p.132).*

November. An especially fine form is 'Fenwick's Variety' with flowers of a richer pink. Dry litter protection – bracken, if you can get it, or straw for example – must be given in winter and you leave the plants undisturbed until the need for division is self-evident. This should be done in July or August, setting the bulbs 4in (10cm) deep.

# 10. Making a Trough Garden

What is it about plants which makes them of such compelling interest? Primarily, I suppose, their perfect proportions, for what exquisite beauty there is in the flowers, say, of a cushion-type saxifrage, the thrift, *Armeria caespitosa*, or a dwarf phlox. All arouse one's protective interest, although they are more than capable of looking after themselves given anything like the right conditions.

And there is no question that, as a patio gardener, you are on an equal footing with anyone else in what you can achieve. You don't need much space for this kind of gardening. A trough

*The interest provided by a trough garden can be immense.*

garden or two also look very handsome in the setting of a patio garden. If planted with skill and care these will look attractive as well when nothing is in flower, but it is, of course, for the succession of colour they can provide that one gives them garden space.

Real stone sinks are now hard to lay one's hands on but manufactured substitutes are easy to obtain and old stone kitchen sinks with glazed surfaces are still occasionally available and quite acceptable if the surface is "doctored", faced with hypertufa. What you should avoid doing at all costs is to grow alpine and rock plants in plastic containers, for these heat up far too much in hot weather and get excessively cold in frosty conditions.

With this kind of container gardening again you must also make sure that the drainage is really good, and this means having at least one hole in the base if the trough is small, and more if it is larger. The internal depth of the trough must also be at least 6in (15cm) and nearer a foot for preference. Each drainage hole should be covered with a piece of perforated zinc to stop insects creeping into the trough, before covering this again with a layer of small crocks (pieces of broken pot), weathered ashes or small stones. Then cover this with a layer of fibrous roughage before adding the compost in which the plants will grow.

**Preparing the container**
But what compost should be used? I have tried several mixtures over the years, some better than others, but I am going to pass on, with his permission, two recipes which my good friend Mr Royton E. Heath, an outstandingly successful alpine plant specialist of amateur status, has found the best through long experience. For sun-loving alpine and rock garden plants he uses a mixture of equal parts loam, leaf-mould and sharp sand; for shade lovers, a mixture of equal parts loam, leaf-mould, peat and sharp sand. Finish off with a sprinkling of lime-free stone chippings in the ordinary way, to help keep the roots of the plant cool and conserve moisture in warm weather.

If you are growing lime-loving plants, too, it is a good idea to add a top-dressing of limestone chippings. Rock plants in general detest winter wet and you can ensure even better drainage of whatever compost you use if you mix in a smattering of broken crocks of very small size – if you happen to have any broken clay pots lying around.

Again, although these plants do not need feeding in the accepted sense, just a sprinkling of bone-meal added to the compost will not come amiss for this will provide extra phosphate over a long period. One has to remember that with this kind of planting an awful lot of roots are competing for a very limited amount of space.

A few small rocks can be added for effect, and there are some

Gentiana verna *'Angulosa'*
*(right)*.

Dianthus *'La Bourbrille'*
*(far right, see p.* 140*)*.

small plants which will grow all the better for the quicker root drainage proximity to these will ensure – cushion plants like the very pretty little white encrusted saxifrage, *Saxifraga cochlearis* 'Minor', a treat for the eye in May, and some of the late spring flowering androsaces. In April the flowers of the cushion-forming drabas arrive – lovely things like *Draba bryoides imbricata* with yellow blooms on the slenderest of stems.

Raise your sink, or sinks, off the ground to ensure that excess water can get away freely. This also serves the very useful purpose of bringing the plants nearer to normal eye level.

Usually you will want to find a sheltered home for the sink in a sunny part of the patio, but you could of course deliberately choose a site with less favourable light conditions. I would suggest leaving that to the more specialised gardener, though, and concentrate on those plants which do like sunshine. That is the vast majority.

### What plants to grow
What to grow is, of course, the next thing you will want to know. A wealth of rock plants and small bulbous plants are admirably suited for this kind of cultivation, and I will make a few suggestions which I hope will prove helpful for troughs in sunny positions.

To begin with there is the thrift, *Armeria caespitosa*, a charming little plant when its cushion growths are covered in May with almost stemless pink blooms. Also, for flowering at the same time, the pretty mat-forming *Phlox douglasii* 'Snow Queen' which, as its name implies, has pure white flowers; and *Erodium reichardii* 'Roseum' (formerly *E. chamaedryoides* 'Roseum'), a very attractive sight when carrying its deep pink flowers just above an inch-high (2.5cm) spread of fresh green small leaves. This is also the time when that lovely gentian, *Gentiana verna* 'Angulosa',

**Opposite:** Narcissus
bulbocodium, *the pretty
hoop-petticoat daffodil, for
February-March flowering
(see p.* 143*).*

A representation of a tiny backyard only 15ft (4.5m) across. There are times when it is necessary to hide something from view, even in a garden of this size, such as, perhaps, a back entrance door, and an alternative to a trellis screen could be a panel of precast concrete screen blocks similar to those shown here. The containers forms an integral part of the design.

flowers, bearing rich blue star-shaped blooms with great aplomb. I recommend, too, the rhizomatous *Oxalis adenophylla* which bears pinkish-mauve flowers on 2 to 3in (5 to 8cm) stems in May and June against grey-coloured foliage.

In summer comes the aromatic little thyme, *Thymus doerfleri*, with deep pink flowers on 1in (2.5cm) stems; the little bellflower, *Campanula arvatica* with violet blooms, and that excellent dianthus, *D.* 'La Bourbrille' with clear pink flowers, prettily displayed against a mat of grey foliage. And, of course, there are

This garden is 52ft (16m) long and 60ft (18m) wide, and the traditional or period house imposes restrictions on the layout. The small, symmetrical house, indeed, calls for a symmetrical response from the designer. In this design there is very little bed space and what there is is raised so that, should the soil be poor, deep excavation and the making of beds would be avoided. The centre panel would, however, need at least 6 to 9in (15 to 23cm) of good soil to support a small lawn. Containers or sinks are placed against the side walls or fences and a single ornament makes a focal point on the lawn.

numerous other dianthus which could be planted as well. Just a mention, too, of the violet- and orange-flowered *Linaria alpina* whose effectiveness is enhanced by its bluish-grey foliage, and the lavender, mat-forming *Globularia cordifolia*, only 2in (5cm) tall. The easily-grown and very attractive houseleeks or sempervivums are also delightful trough-garden plants; *Sempervivum arachnoideum* and *S. tectorum* and their cultivars are especially recommended.

Miniature roses are other possibilities; these could include

orange-red 'Starina'; lavender-coloured 'Lavender Jewel'; shell-pink 'Dresden Doll', with 'mossed' buds; 'Baby Masquerade', red and yellow; 'Golden Angel', yellow; and 'Pour Toi', cream. See p. 85 for more on miniature roses.

There are many bulbous plants which are ideal for this kind of display – from grape hyacinths (muscari), dwarf crocuses and dwarf narcissi like the exquisite *Narcissus cyclamineus, N. bulbocodium* and *N. triandrus albus* to dwarf irises such as *I. reticulata* and *I. histrioides*, the last bearing its rich blue flowers as early as January. Small tulip species like the yellow- and white-flowered *Tulipa tarda*, which makes its display in April, can also be grown in this way.

A dwarf conifer gives character to a trough garden and by far the most popular for this purpose is the very small growing *Juniperus communis* 'Compressa' with glaucous green foliage. This takes many years to reach a height of 2ft (60cm). A lovely little "bun" conifer is *Chamaecyparis obtusa caespitosa* with rich green foliage, while another is the small and very attractive little conifer *Thuja occidentalis* 'Hetz Midget', globular in shape, dark green in colour and very slow growing.

The Lilliputian world of the trough garden can be a joy. But now a few other cultural details which may help you in your trough gardening. Pot-grown alpine plants can be put in at almost any time during reasonable weather, but spring is an especially good time with the growing season ahead. As with containers of other kinds, be very conscious that they will dry out rapidly in hot, sunny weather and pay attention to their watering needs accordingly. It is a great help to have a layer of stone chipping on the compost's surface to lessen such moisture losses.

There are quite a lot of rock plants which object to winter damp, including the dianthus and the draba I have mentioned; overhead shelter can be provided using a pane of glass attached to a wire frame.

Tulipa tarda

**Opposite:** Linaria alpina *with violet and orange flowers, grows here with* Asperula suberosa *(see p. 141).*

143

# 11. Plants in Paving

Growing rock plants in a sun-bathed paved area has its attractions for the patio gardener. It is as well, though, to go into things quite carefully early on, for the visual effect can be marred if the ratio between plants and paving is not conducive to a basic harmony. Try to imagine what the overall feature will look like when the plants are mature, and endeavour to create a pattern of textures and colours.

A lot of plants do well in these conditions with their roots delving down into cool soil. I particularly like to see the thrift, *Armeria maritima*, grown thus, and a campanula like *G. garganica* with its blue, star-like flowers, provides a lovely show in summer; also the Corsican mint, *Mentha requienii*, with its tiny aromatic leaves, smelling of peppermint, and lilac-mauve flowers in summer.

Gaily coloured rock roses (helianthemums), which make evergreen clumps up to 9in (23cm) high in colours from orange, shades of red, pink and yellow throughout the summer months, are difficult to fault for a sunny site. Numerous dianthuses and aubrietas can also be effectively exploited as well as cultivars of *Saxifraga paniculata* (syn. *S. aizoon*); the cobweb houseleek, *Sempervivum arachnoideum*, and such attractive varieties of the thyme, *Thymus serpyllum*, as 'Pink Chintz'. For summer colour there is also the pretty *Viola cornuta*, with lavender-coloured blooms, and its white cultivar, 'Alba'. Other useful paving plants are the acaenas, and especially *Acaena microphylla*, which has greenish bronze leaves and crimson burrs (seed heads) from mid-summer onwards.

A prostrate juniper like *Juniperus communis* 'Hornibrookii' can also look attractive spreading over paving, for its stems, heavy with little greyish-green leaves, are at a most a foot high, and it has a spread of up to 5ft (1.5m). Perhaps twice as tall and with much the same kind of spread as the last-mentioned in time, is the well-known and excellent *Juniperus sabina tamariscifolia*, with rich green foliage. It is an asset to any garden but much will depend on how much room you have to spare for this kind of thing.

The junipers I have mentioned grow well in most soils, including chalk, and they appreciate plenty of sunshine. So, too, does the colourful *Thuja occidentalis* 'Rheingold' of conical shape,

144

which has foliage of a warm yellow which turns to bronzy-gold in winter. After a long time this may grow as much as 10ft (3m) tall, though it is more likely to be rather less than half that height.

A delightful very slow-growing small spruce, too, for which a planting pocket might be found in a paved area is *Picea abies nidiformis,* which ultimately makes a densely branched, flat-topped bush some 3ft (1m) tall and 5ft (1.5m) wide with dark green colouring. If your garden lies in what is called a frost pocket, though (i.e. cold air drains into it from higher levels), this would not be a good choice as the new growth can be damaged when severe frost occur in early spring. It has the rather delightful common name of bird's nest spruce.

I think that we shall see much more use made of dwarf and slow-growing conifers in paved areas in the years ahead, with, of course, planting pockets of appropriate size being left for them. I remember being very impressed by a paved patio garden which I saw in Switzerland a year or so ago where, apart from climbing and wall shrubs planted against the white house walls, the only plants consisted of dwarf and slow-growing conifers set most attractively among the paving in the way I have just suggested. Most in evidence were forms of the mountain pine of central and south-east Europe, *Pinus mugo,* and very handsome they looked, too. One of the best of these forms, freely available here, is 'Mops' which makes a bun-shaped bush of greyish-green of around 1½ft (45cm) and 2ft (60cm) wide in time. This cultivar is, of course, a great favourite with rock gardening enthusiasts.

I found this small Swiss garden fascinating to see but what I am not sure about is how long it would remain really satisfying if one had to live with it over a period of years – perhaps in its concentration on one type of plant it is just too much of a good

*When planting paved areas, the aim should be to create a pattern of pleasing textures and colours.*

The pretty little herbaceous
Geranium cinereum
'Ballerina' which flowers in the
first half of summer.

thing. Its real interest lies in the stimulus it gives to devote, say, part of a paved area to this kind of display. Dwarf conifers certainly have impact, especially if you can emulate the kind of picture I have tried to draw. And the maintenance needed, of course, is minimal, which, if you are either extremely busy or not too active, could be a consideration.

Do not overlook either the use of prostrate shrubs such as *Cotoneaster dammeri* with its bright red berries or the 3ft (1m) tall *C. conspicuus* 'Decorus', also extremely free-berrying. Both of these are described on p. 57. The smaller growing potentillas I have discussed on pp. 46 and 48 would also be admirable for the purpose in question, and the charming little herbaceous geranium, 'Ballerina'.

But whatever plants you use for planting in a paved area, remember my earlier advice to keep the ratio between plants and paving in balance.

# 12. Annuals for a Quick Display

There are numerous annuals, many of them half-hardy – those you can't plant out until the danger of frost has passed – which you can put to good use as container-grown plants for summer display. And if you have no greenhouse for raising the half-hardies yourself, you can always buy young plants by the box in late May and early June. However, I would suggest that you take a look at some of the really small and neat lean-to greenhouses available nowadays for they are certainly of a size suitable for a patio setting. Bedding plants can now be quite costly to buy and raising your own is also great fun. You can make sowings of half-hardy annuals in a warm greenhouse from late February to April providing a germinating temperature of about 15°C (59°F) –earlier sowing is not usually necessary – or in a cold greenhouse or frame in late March and April. The resulting plants must not be planted out in the garden until late May or early June, after hardening-off.

Of course, you can easily provide for some delightful splashes of summer colour around the patio by sowing seeds of hardy annuals between late March and early May in whatever pockets of spare ground you happen to have available, provided they are open to a fair bit of sunshine.

## Summer bedding

Again, you can buy in young plants of half-hardy annuals as I have just suggested (or raise them yourself) and enjoy a fine display, for little trouble, if you make border plantings of things like the brightly coloured impatiens (busy lizzies) – strains such as 'Super Elfin' and 'Accent' – which do well in light shade, French and African marigolds, petunias, cultivars of *Phlox drummondii*, lobelias, antirrhinums and asters of various kinds, salvias, nemesias, ursinias and zinnias.

Another half-hardy plant which is extremely attractive and used for summer bedding is the fibrous-rooted begonia (the *semperflorens* type) which is available in wide variety and in heights from 6in to 1ft (15 to 30cm) depending on the strain.

Phlox drummondii

147

These plants are extremely free-flowering and are in bloom from July until October. My favourite strain is 'Organdy', some 6in (15cm) tall, always very eye-catching and with colours from red and pink in various shades to white. It is very resistant to wet weather. The leaf colouring can be either green or bronze. Of special interest are 'Danica Scarlet' and 'Danica Rose', rosy-red, 14in (35cm) tall hybrids which have larger flowers than the general run of these plants, attractive bronze foliage and good weather resistance. All the fibrous begonias of this type give a fine display of colour, with flowers ranging from orangy-red to scarlet, salmon and pink to white.

Then, of course, there are the annual pinks (dianthus), lovely flowers for a sunny, well-drained position, especially the 6in (15cm) tall Magic Charms strain which includes colours like crimson, pink, salmon and white as well as bicolours; multi-coloured dahlias like the well-known Coltness Hybrids and strains like Dandy and Redskin with flowers of numerous colours; and the brilliantly coloured (orange, red and yellow) *Tagetes signata pumila* cultivars which are so excellent for edging beds.

### Growing from seed

I must make particular mention of the intermediate-sized strain of sweet pea named Jet Set. The significance of it is that the modestly sized plants, only 3ft (1m) tall, bear a wealth of blooms whose size and length and sturdiness of stem match up to that of the traditional tall Spencer-type cultivars. The colours include scarlet, crimson, cerise, salmon, mauve, blue and cream. You can grow these Jet Sets from a spring sowing made where the plants are to flower. With that kind of stature one can think of many uses for them in the patio garden, and of course, like all sweet peas, they are in a class of their own as cut flowers, both for their beauty of form and colour and their fragrance.

These Jet Sets are an improved strain of the Knee-Hi sweet peas which have become popular in recent years, and need only the support of short sticks or netting to keep them in trim. Of much the same stature is the Little Elf strain and shorter by far are the Patio and Dwarf Bijiou strains for these are little over 1ft (30cm) tall. A quite different sweet pea is 'Snoopea' 2ft (60cm) tall and without the usual tendrils, and the improved form of this, 'Supersnoop', with larger flowers in a wide range of colours. This makes a good border plant with its fine range of colour and pleasant fragrance.

Sweet peas like the sun, of course, and need a deeply dug soil with plenty of humus-forming material in it so that they do not lack moisture at the roots.

If you can provide a sunny spot where the soil is poor there is nothing like the nasturtiums – hardy annuals you sow in April or May. Climbing or trailing, the typical tall, 6 to 8ft (2 to 2.5m)

Dahlia *Coltness Hybrids*

nasturium with its single blooms, in shades of red, orange and yellow, is a considerable asset from July to September, and so are the double-flowered semi-tall and dwarf kinds which have heights of 15in (38cm) and 6 to 9in (15 to 23cm) respectively, and are very useful for bedding. Particularly good are the semi-tall Gleam hybrids and the Jewel Mixed dwarfs, which carry their very colourful flowers well above the foliage. 'Empress of India' with crimson flowers and dark foliage can look especially gay if it is given the contrast of a white background. The typical back spur of the flower is missing from the dwarf 'Whirlybird', a free-flowering mixture in which the flowers of various colours face upwards on top of the stems and above the foliage to create a very colourful show. Give nasturtiums (tropaeolum is, of course, their botanical name) too good a soil and the flowers will be drowned by the foliage, so lushly will they grow – the poorer the better in this case.

One of my favourite hardy annuals is *Layia elegans,* called tidy tips, which bears showy daisy flowers for most of the summer. It is really a very pretty plant, its blooms having a centre of deep yellow surrounded by golden-yellow ray-florets, which are tipped with white. With a height of about 1½ft (45cm) it is useful in the patio garden and the blooms last well when cut for the house. Another favourite of mine is *Limnanthes douglasii,* a lovely sprawling plant from north-west America which produces a

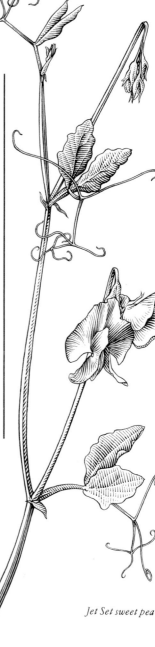

*Jet Set sweet pea*

mass of white flowers with yellow centres to earn itself the rather amusing name of poached egg-flower. It is especially good for planting beside a low flight of steps which it can ''invade'', and it is very good value as it flowers from early in summer to August. You can sow the seeds where the plants are to flower in September or in March, with the September planting, of course, giving earlier flowering.

*Annual flowers providing a riot of colour.*

You can sow seeds of the Californian poppy, eschscholzia, and godetia (also, as it happens, a Californian native) in September if you wish, but March or April is the more usual sowing time. September sowing brings earlier flower but it means taking a chance that there will not be abnormally bad weather conditions in winter.

Two goods strains of eschscholzia, both about 1ft (30cm) tall,

151

are Harlequin and Ballerina. The colour range is good and the flowers are either double or semi-double. By far the best known and most popular godetia is 'Sybil Sherwood', a truly delightful cultivar with salmon-pink, white-edged blooms which are borne in abundance. This also is about 1ft (30cm) tall and so admirable for narrow patio borders. Alternatively, you could decide that the slightly taller Azalea-flowered strain with an excellent range of colours would be preferable. The blooms do resemble those of azaleas, so the name has relevance.

Two hardy annuals of unusual distinction are *Lavatera* 'Silver Cup' and *L.* 'Mont Blanc'. Both are some 2ft (60cm) tall and literally smother their bushy frames with the highly attractive, trumpet-shaped single blooms. Those of 'Silver Cup' are rose-pink with silvery shading; those of 'Mont Blanc' pure white. Their cultivation is of the easiest, the seeds being sown where the plants are to flower at any time in spring. In importance I would rate them with the three rudbeckias whose descriptions follow.

### Resistance to bad weather

Some of the finest and most exciting new flowers from seed to be introduced for years are the rudbeckias 'Marmalade', 'Rustic Dwarfs' and 'Goldilocks' which, from a sowing made in a heated greenhouse in February or March will provide plants for setting out after all danger of frost has passed in late May or early June to provide colour from July into autumn. Alternatively, seeds can be sown between April to June to give plants for setting out in autumn or in the following spring. Both 'Marmalade' and 'Rustic Dwarfs' make plants about 1½ft (45cm) tall which smother themselves with the most striking ray flowers – in the first case rich golden-yellow and in the second case in shades of mahogany-red, bronze, golden and yellow. The flowers of 'Marmalade' are up to 5in (13cm) across, those of 'Rustic Dwarfs' if anything slightly more. 'Goldilocks' is taller (about 2ft or 60cm) and has semi-double golden-yellow flowers which are very showy. They make excellent cut flowers for the house. One other thing of

Rudbeckia *'Rustic Dwarfs'*

152

importance: they stand up remarkably well to bad weather – an important factor in our climate!

If you are using petunias for bedding or for growing in containers (and what better!) take note than the Resisto strain, of which there is a dwarf section, has especially weather-resistant blooms. To see them against other petunias in a wet spell shows this up clearly. These, like other petunias, you can sow up till the end of March in a heated greenhouse to provide plants, duly hardened off, for planting out in a sunny part of the garden in late May or early June.

I have been impressed also by the performance of the handsome cultivar of the perennial *Coreopsis grandiflora* named 'Sunray'. Masses of double, golden-yellow blooms are borne on a plant 18in (45cm) tall. By sowing seed under glass early in the year (February or March) and setting the plants out in May, flowering will take place from July onwards. This is another plant which performs well in wet weather and the blooms are excellent for cutting.

A 4ft (1.3m) sunflower (helianthus), too, like 'Autumn Sunshine', with flowers in shades of yellow and red, can create a good impression, if well placed. And, at the other end of the scale, a sweet william like 'Wee Willy', only 6in (15cm) tall, can be just right for edging a small plant bed. It is a biennial, but you grow it as a hardy annual or as half-hardy annual if you wish.

There is something especially satisfying about growing plants like this from seed. One thing we can all appreciate is the quick results which annuals give. It is possible to experiment with different plants and plant combinations to one's heart content.

### Other plants of distinction

Another superb plant which won a Fleuroselect bronze medal in 1978 and which has made its presence felt increasingly since then is *Salvia farinacea* 'Victoria', really a perennial but grown as a half-hardy annual. From a base of arched rich green leaves arise bold spikes of purplish-blue flowers to a height of about 2ft (60cm). Its makes an ideal companion for many other plants, and not only annuals.

Another group of half-hardy annuals which has come much to the fore in recent years is the nicotianas or tobacco plants, notable for their fragrance (especially in the evenings) and in quite a few modern hybrids and strains opening up their flowers in the daytime and not in the evening only, as is the nicotiana's natural inclination. These have heights of between 1ft (30cm) or even a little less and 3ft (1m), as in the case of the highly scented 'Evening Fragrance' mixture in which are found shades of purple, mauve, red, pink and white. 'Lime Green' is a firm favourite, especially with the flower arrangers, for it has pale yellowish-

green flowers which associate beautifully with the flowers of many other plants, being borne on 2ft (60cm) stems.

The 2½ft (75cm) tall Sensation mixture also has an excellent colour range and makes a telling feature in the right situation. Much smaller at 1ft (30cm) is the Nicki mixture, also with a good colour range and the kind of stature which makes it very useful in the confines of a patio garden. The same can be said of the Domino mixture which is of much the same height. Sensation, Nicki and Domino mixtures all open their flowers in the daytime.

I would rate the pretty, extremely free-flowering nemesias among the finest of half-hardy annuals for patio gardening (or for use in any garden for that matter). The funnel-shaped blooms come in numerous attractive colours and in the delightful Carnival mixture are borne on stems no more than 7 to 8in (18 to 20cm) high. The colours of this strain range from orange and red to pink, pale yellow and white. I personally prefer the compact kinds to the rather taller ones with a height of 1ft (30cm) or thereabouts, but all are marvellous plants for bedding purposes.

**Above:** *For providing colour from mid-summer onwards, few seed-raised plants can beat the petunias, in containers or beds.*

**Opposite:** Rudbeckia *'Marmalade', one of the most significant and colourful plants in the seedsmen's lists.*

# 13. Something for the Table

It can be great fun to use a little space in even a small garden to grow a few fruits and vegetables, especially the latter, and I want to just briefly discuss the possibilities in this direction, using any spare bit of ground or containers you may have.

**Vegetables and salad crops**

Vegetables first, for growing these is an interest of so many people these days. Very popular indeed is growing tomatoes outdoors, even though you have got to have the weather on your side to achieve the best results. It is a gamble well worth taking, and you will naturally set aside a really warm, sheltered spot in which to grow the plants, either a bed or a container, where they will get all the sunshine which is going.

If you do not have the facilities to raise your own plants from seed you will buy hardened off plants at the end of May or in early June for immediate planting, not before the latter date in colder parts of the country. Prepare the ground well in advance of this and dig in either some well-decayed farmyard manure (if you can get it) or garden compost and make sure that the soil is well drained.

Set the plants 1½ft (45cm) apart in the row and don't plant too deeply. Have something like ½in (1cm) of soil over the ball of roots. Stake at the time of planting and take out the side shoots so that the plant is kept to a single stem. Then, when the third or fourth flower truss has formed pinch out the tip of the leading shoot. Start to feed regularly with a proprietary tomato feed when the first fruits begin to develop, and make sure that they get enough water. All the fruit must be gathered before the frost occurs, and any which are still green ripened in boxes in a warm room.

Bush varieties like ''The Amateur'' and $F_1$ hybirds like 'Alfresco', 'Red Alert' and 'Totem' (compact and especially good for patio cultivation) do not need pinching out, of course. A quite recent introduction of special interest to the patio gardener is the cultivar 'Minibel' which bears quantities of quite small fruits of good quality on a plant 1ft (30cm) tall. It performs well as a pot-grown plant and is excellent, of course, for cultivating in growing bags, as is 'Totem', in particular.

Other varieties for outdoors include 'Outdoor Girl' and 'Sweet 100' which bears masses of small, sweetly flavoured fruits.

Very convenient for the patio gardener are the proprietary growing bags which I alluded to above. These are filled with specially formulated soil-less compost in which crops like tomatoes, runner beans, marrows, herbs and flowers can be grown with ease. They can increase your growing area very appreciably.

If you want to try your hand at growing some runner beans make a sowing in mid-May in a rather rich soil which is well supplied with moisture. Sow the seed 2in (5cm) deep and 9in (23cm) apart in a single row or a double row 1ft (30cm) apart. In preparation for this it is advisable to dig the ground over deeply at least a couple of months beforehand and add some well-decayed manure at that time if it can be obtained, or garden compost. If you are not supporting your runner beans on trellis work or setting against a wall or fence, stake the plants very early on with long poles, and make quite sure that the plants are getting plenty of moisture at the roots during the flowering period and when the pods are developing. A peat mulch applied in early summer will be very helpful in conserving soil moisture. Two excellent varieties are 'Scarlet Emperor' and 'Streamline'. Pick the pods as soon as they become ready, and you should get a good three months of supply from your plants from July onwards.

But don't be over-hasty about getting in the seeds for this is a frost-sensitive vegetable. It is excellent, too, for container growing if you cannot manage to find a bit of spare ground.

If you have a warm, sunny corner spare where the soil is of really good quality what better crop to grow, too, than small bush Courgette marrows, which you cut for use when about 6in (15cm) long. This way you catch this vegetable at its most succulent and it encourages better cropping. Sow the seeds at the end of May or in early June where the plants are to be grown in rich soil laced with well-rotted manure or garden compost if you have no facility for raising plants under glass. This is another crop which needs much moisture and the watering must be watched, particularly in dry weather. It pays to hand fertilise the female flowers with the male flowers to ensure a good crop. (The female flowers have an unformed marrow behind them, which shows as a swollen area.)

How rewarding it can be, too, to give a little ground to lettuces, sowing little and often to provide a succession over many months. (With cloche protection and a greenhouse in which to raise plants it is possible to have lettuces the year round, but I'm not thinking on those ambitious lines.) To get the quick growth which is needed you should grow lettuces in good soil

*The bush marrow 'Golden Zucchini'.*

with excellent moisture-retaining properties while still being well-drained. The plants must never be allowed to suffer from lack of moisture. Grow them also in a position open to plenty of sunshine.

Good butterhead cultivars of the cabbage type include 'Tom Thumb' (for March-April sowing), a very useful small-headed kind; 'Salad Bowl' (for sowing from April to July) and the excellent 'Avondefiance' for sowing from June to early August.

*The excellent butterhead lettuce 'Salad Bowl' for sowing from April to July.*

An extremely useful cos lettuce is 'Little Gem' (it is a compact-growing cultivar which is part cos and part cabbage lettuce in appearance) and this is suitable for sowing outdoors from March to mid-summer. Another good cos variety is 'Lobjoit's Green Cos'. Sow seeds ½in (1cm) deep in rows set 12in (30cm) apart and thin out the resulting seedling to 9 to 12in (23 to 30cm) apart in the rows.

Again, you could consider growing radishes and onions for

salad use. Both give an excellent return for the small amount of ground they take up.

Little and often is definitely the rule with radish sowings (as with lettuces) for this is a crop which needs to be grown well and quickly for use as required. To achieve this you need to make the sowings in soil of good quality and with good moisture-retentive qualities (or you must watch the need for water with special care).

Make successional sowings of radishes outdoors as often as once a fortnight (or at a little longer interval than that, depending on your need) from March until August. (Earlier sowings than that can be made, of course, with glass protection, and there are winter-hardy varieties for sowing in July and August, but we won't go into that here). For the sowings I've suggested, consider growing such varieties as the well-known 'French Breakfast', 'Cherry Belle', 'Scarlet Globe' or 'Long White Icicle'.

Sow the seeds in drills ¼ in (0.5cm) deep and with 5 to 6in (13 to 15cm) between the rows. Sow thinly. Never let the plants be checked in growth through lack of water at the roots. Water as necessary. Very light shade is needed for summer crops of radish but sunny positions for the early crops.

'White Lisbon' is the variety of onion to grow for salad purposes, and you can make successional sowings from March to June in drills set 9in to 1ft (23 to 30cm) apart. Sow thinly and pull the resulting onions as they reach the required size and are needed. You can also make a sowing in July or August of 'White Lisbon – Winter Hardy' to provide onions for pulling in spring.

Lastly, a little bit of fun: growing first-early potatoes in a tub or other large container, in John Innes No. 3 potting compost or some other really good growing mixture of your own concoction. Plant the tubers (after sprouting them in a frost-proof, well-ventilated place open to good light) in late March or early April. If you want to do the equivalent of mounding up the potatoes later, then only just over half-fill the container with compost and add more as top growth develops. Otherwise, start off with more compost and keep the light away from the tubers by letting the plants grow through a covering of black polythene.

Any first-early variety can be grown in this way, and, as always nowadays, with most seed potatoes being obtained locally, it is a question of making a choice from thoses on offer. Naturally, you will want to plant a first-early variety for the novelty has gone out of the operation once there are plenty of new potatoes around. Earliness is the thing.

## Herbs

Now a few words about herbs, which are useful in the kitchen and can be grown in odd corners of the garden. Parsley is something it is always useful to have around and it is usual to make two sowings a year, where the plants are to mature: the first in March or April, the second in late June or July. The seeds take five or even more weeks to germinate so don't expect results too quickly. The soil should be kept moist at this time. Sow in drills ¼ in (0.5cm) deep and thin the resulting seedlings to 6in (15cm) apart. At the end of the season you could cover some of the plants from the second sowing with a cloche. The best-known cultivar is 'Moss Curled'.

The common thyme, *Thymus vulgaris*, makes a bush a foot high and likes a sunny position and a well-drained, preferably limy soil. Sow seeds in March and thin the resulting seedlings to 12in (30cm) apart. You can also raise plants of pot marjoram, *Origanum onites*, from a sowing made in May, but it is better to buy young plants and put these in in spring, 1ft (30cm) apart. This herb likes a moist, well-drained soil.

Mint is useful but it does spread, especially when given the conditions it likes – sunshine, and a rather rich, moist soil – and for that reason some gardeners like to grow it in a container, just to keep it within bounds. Buy plants for spring or autumn planting.

**Top fruit**

Now to fruit. As I remarked earlier you could consider growing the Morello cherry as a fan-trained specimen against a north-facing wall if you have such available. All it really needs to do well is good drainage and a soil well-supplied with lime. An espalier trained apple or pear could be grown against a wall facing south or south-west if you have 10 to 15ft (3 to 4.5cm) of clear space and the soil is loamy and well-drained and there is reasonable shelter from winds. You could also grow cordon apples or pears against a wall or fence of similar aspect.

As I remarked earlier there is no reason why you shouldn't have a "family tree", with three varieties of dessert apples or three varieties of pears grafted on to the one bush, all carefully chosen to have matching flowering periods and readily cross-pollinating one another. It must be understood, however, that such bushes will have a height of 12 to 15ft (3.8 to 4.5m) eventually. It is interesting to note, for instance, that two excellent new apple varieties are among the varieties obtainable in this way – 'Merton Knave', a nicely flavoured dessert variety which matures from late August to mid-September, and 'Spartan', a variety of especially good eating quality which can be eaten straight from the tree or to be kept until Christmas (its season is October to December). You can have a bush on which the varieties 'Merton Knave', 'Egremont Russett' and 'Golden Delicious' have been worked, or, alternatively, 'James Grieve', 'Spartan' and 'Cox's Orange Pippin'. There are numerous other combinations of apples available in addition to the two mentioned, mostly dessert cultivars but one selection all cookers and another two dessert

and one cooker. I have used as examples combination offered by Highfield Nurseries, Whitminster, Gloucester. They are also offering on one bush the pears 'Williams' Bon Chrétien', 'Conference' and 'Doyenné du Comice'. Between them, these

*'Cox's Orange Pippin', the
aristocrat of dessert apples
which is in season from October
to early January. It is only
suitable, however, for growing
in good conditions (in other than
cold gardens) and is prone to
attack by canker and mildew.
'Sunset', with something
of Cox's quality and
flavour without the draw-
backs, is an attractive
alternative. It is in season
from October to mid-December'.*

apples and pears provide a succession of fruit over the period
August to March. Other fruit specialists offer other combinations,
and family trees are available also through selected garden
centres.

### New developments

Before the sweet cherry 'Stella' arrived on the scene in the early 1970s – bred at a research station in British Columbia – there was no self-fertile sweet cherry. 'Stella' is still, at the time of writing, the only self-fertile cultivar of its type. Morever, it is now married to the semi-vigorous rootstock Colt and, for the first time, it is possible to think of growing a sweet cherry, within reasonable space, in a small garden and with no need to provide another compatible pollinating cultivar.

Even with 'Stella' on Colt, however, you will have a bush or half-standard tree with an eventual height of around 20ft (6cm), and the answer in the patio garden is to grow this cultivar as a fan-trained specimen. All that is needed then is a tall wall with room for the cherry to have a lateral spread of 15ft (4.5m). 'Stella' is vigorous with an upright habit and throws laterals in a manner very suitable for training.

'Stella' is certainly worth finding space for, for, in the summer of 1982, it won the accolade of a first class certificate from the Royal Horticultural Society – a high award given sparingly at the best of times and hardly ever to a fruit. Its large, dark red fruits, which have good flavour, ripen in late July and it is a heavy cropper. Another point in its favour is that it has good resistance to bacterial canker, which is a serious trouble of cherries. It is something to think about, if you have the space available against a south- or west-facing wall. But remember that sweet cherries need a good, well-drained soil to grow in, and plenty of moisture in the soil, especially when the fruits are developing. The latest development is a more compact narrower form of 'Stella', named 'Compact Stella', from the same Canadian source which Highfield are the first to offer. This has obvious possibilties for patio cultivation.

An extremely dwarfing apple rootstock, M27, has been developed at the Institute of Horticultural Research, East Malling, Maidstone, Kent, of which more in a moment, and a dwarfing rootstock for plums named Pixy, of special interest to all gardeners with an enthusiasm for fruit growing but space problems of one kind or another.

Highfield Nurseries (referred to on p. 162 in connection with family trees of apples and pears) developed a few years ago a novel form of training for the self-fertile dessert plum 'Victoria' worked onto Pixy rootstock – "festooning", as they call it. It has real practical advantages in increasing fruitfulness, and is of special interest to patio gardeners, who want every plant given space to realise its full potential. The system works equally well with apples grown on certain dwarfing rootstocks, but more of that in a moment.

It is a good method to adopt whether you are growing the fruits just mentioned in a bed or in large containers.

But first the plum 'Victoria' grown on Pixy rootstock, which

This garden at the corner of a road is about 60ft (18m) square, and the entrance through the wrought iron gate is screened from the drawing room window by a narrow yew hedge. This also serves as a backcloth for the sculpture on the edge of the small pool. If so desired, the pool could be a plant bed, but water adds greatly to the attractions of small patio gardens of this type. The curved, raised bed adjoining the water feature would make an admirable home for alpine and rock plants. The small conifer helps the yew hedge to screen the sitting-out area from the gate. Note how the tree interrupts the line of the wall and so counters effectively the sense of enclosure which this induces.

165

makes trees up to two-thirds the size of those on the much-used St. Julien A rootstock. (Another different but very interesting development is that this rootstock has made it possible to grow plums as cordons, with 'Victoria' again highly suitable for the purpose).

Essentially, festooning consists of taking a two-year-old tree with a framework of three or four branches and bending these branches down and securing them to the stem. The objective is to divert the tree's energies into the formation and development of fruit buds rather than have it make excessive branch growth ('Victoria' is strong growing). Indeed, the system often induces such prolific fruiting that thinning of the fruitlets is necessary to get fruits of acceptable size (with small fruits the stone comprises most of the volume).

Under the Highfield system the laterals on the main branches are reduced in length by almost half a year or so later, this pruning being done in late summer with the cuts being made back to a bud in each case. New branches which have developed since the original training can, if so desired, be similarly "festooned".

They also recommend festooning some branches on older trees if these are making excessive growth to the detriment of fruit production. Try it, if you have a tree which is not performing as it should do, and so achieve a better balance between growth and fruiting.

Highfield have shown, too, that it is possible to stimulate increased fruit production by festooning apple varieties worked onto the very dwarfing M27 rootstock – not suitable for weak-growing varieties – and the dwarfing M9 rootstock. I would emphasies, however, that apples grown on M27 and M9 must be grown in really good soil, and in John Innes No 3 potting compost if they are grown in containers (this also applies to plum 'Victoria' grown in this way). The apples should be fed also in the growing season with a fertiliser with a high potash content. Such bushes need the support of stakes throughout their lives. Those grown in containers will also need to have the top inch or so of compost replaced each spring with fresh compost of the same type after the first year.

The space-saving benefits these rootstocks confer are real. The M27 rootstock provides a bush at maturity of around 5ft (1.5m) in height and similar spread, while M9 gives a bush some 8 to 9ft (2.4 to 2.7m) tall and wide. Fruiting starts early, too, normally in the third year from planting and often in two years in the case of bushes on M27, and the fruits are often better coloured than those on rootstocks making larger bushes or trees.

Don't overlook the necessity of ensuring efficient cross-pollination with apples, for, while many are self-fertile, all will give better crops with cross-pollination, and some are self-sterile and will bear no fruit at all without this facility. So, whatever variety you choose to grow should have a compatible variety near

The rear of a country cottage modernised by the addition of a patio in simple rectangular slabs and a brick-edged cobbled area containing an abstract sculpture. Three shallow, easily negotiated steps lead down to the small lawn in the foreground. The sitting-out area is kept free of draughts by the wall leading from the corner of the house, this containing a door to another part of the garden.

The tree on the patio is a Malus or flowering crab, but it could be, just as suitably, a variety of Sorbus aucuparia (mountain ash), a laburnum or a flowering cherry. The steps are heavily planted with a selection of rock plants and good ground-cover plants such as Vinca (periwinkle) and Ajuga (bugle). A way up and down the steps is provided by the single slab on each step.

variety you choose to grow should have a compatible variety near by which shares its flowering period, early, mid-season or late, and will allow cross-pollination – the transfer of pollen and subsequent fertilisation. There is no problem about what to plant with what for the catalogues of fruit specialists give advice on the compatibility of the varieties they offer, whether it is apples, pears, cherries or plums in which you are interested.

**Soft fruit**
The new high yielding autumn fruiting raspberry. 'Autumn Bliss', is a good choice for growing in large containers, cropping being much heavier than that of other autumn fruiting varieties over a period from mid-August to the end of September. Grow in John Innes No. 3 potting compost.

Of the summer-fruiting raspberries for planting in a bed, a good choice would be the early cultivar 'Glen Moy' for July cropping and 'Leo' for August cropping. Raspberries do well in sunshine or light shade in a soil which should be fertile and moisture-retentive but well drained.

Most people like strawberries, and the best way to grow these is in the ground, but if this is not possible they can be grown very satisfactorily in 9in (23cm) pots on the patio, when they will give a good yield (or in barrels or other containers). Use John Innes No. 3 potting compost for this purpose. The whole range of strawberry varieties can be grown in this way. Two cultivars of particular interest for this purpose are the Dutch-raised summer-fruiting 'Tamella' and the perpetual (or remontant) variety 'Ostara'. 'Tamella' is a high-yielding cultivar which can be used for dessert, freezing, jam-making or bottling–'Ostara' (also Dutch-raised), like others of its kind, fruits early (in June) and again later in the season (August to October). To keep up the yield it is best only to leave strawberries in containers for the one year. Plant container-grown strawberries in August or early September even though planting can go on into autumn, just as with those grown in the open ground. It is best to get the job done as soon as possible. Remember also that strawberries should be grown in a sunny position.

With pot-grown plants, pot them in August, and with the arrival of winter turn the pots on their sides to avoid the compost becoming too wet. In early February turn the pots right side up and when growth begins start to water, increasing the amounts given as the plants develop. You can grow strawberries in this way without any glass protection at all.

Tiered pots are available for strawberry growing called Tower-pots, these being made of polypropylene and locking together to make a column of 4 pots with 12 planting stations. Modern versions of the traditional strawberry barrel are also available.

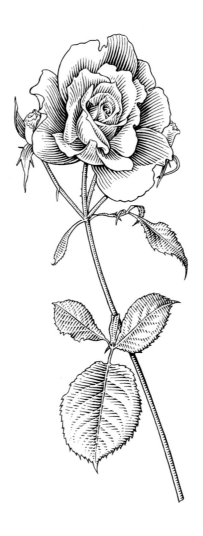

# Afterword

A cynic once said that gardening books tell you everything except the answer to the problem which is plaguing you at the moment. There is a grain of truth in this, alas, for with a subject so broad and with so many fascinating facets and byways the author's problem is what to leave out rather than what to put in, even when the subject matter is as specific as it is in this case.

What I have attempted to do more than anything else is to give you ideas, to set you thinking by bringing to your notice a host of good garden plants. Some, at least, should match your tastes and the kind of garden you have been hoping to create. For a garden is a very personal possession; it provides opportunities for self-expression and personal fulfilment which are difficult to describe in words. It is a mirror of yourself.

Gardening is the most rewarding of pastimes, whether you have the smallest of plots or something more ambitious, and a patio garden, with its intimate atmosphere, can be a haven of delight. If you haven't had it already, I hope you will soon have confirmation of that through your own experiences.

# Index

*(Page numbers in italics indicate illustrations)*